LOVING STYLES

DR. MARTIN F. ROSENMAN, *a resident of Atlanta, is an associate professor of psychology at Morehouse College and a practicing clinical psychologist who specializes in the relationships between men and women.*

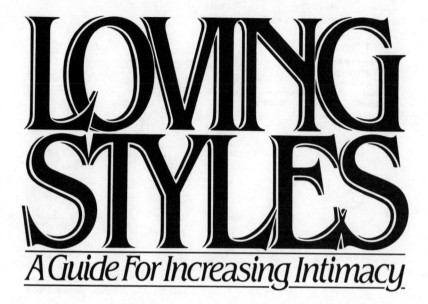

LOVING STYLES

A Guide For Increasing Intimacy

MARTIN F. ROSENMAN

PRENTICE-HALL, INC., *Englewood Cliffs, N.J.* 07632

A SPECTRUM BOOK

Library of Congress Cataloging in Publication Data

ROSENMAN, MARTIN F
  Loving Styles.

  (A Spectrum Book)
  Bibliography: p.
  Includes index.
  1. Love. 2. Intimacy (Psychology) I. Title.
BF575.L8R67   158'.2   79-20502
ISBN 0-13-541052-5
ISBN 0-13-541045-2 pbk.

© 1979 by Prentice-Hall, Inc.
Englewood Cliffs, New Jersey 07632

A SPECTRUM BOOK

3 4 5 6 7 8 9 10

Printed in the United States of America

Editorial/production supervision and
interior design by Norma Miller Karlin
Cover design by Tony Ferrara Studio, Inc.
Manufacturing buyer: Cathie Lenard

PRENTICE-HALL INTERNATIONAL, INC., *London*
PRENTICE-HALL OF AUSTRALIA PTY. LIMITED, *Sydney*
PRENTICE-HALL OF CANADA, LTD., *Toronto*
PRENTICE-HALL OF INDIA PRIVATE LIMITED, *New Delhi*
PRENTICE-HALL OF JAPAN, INC., *Tokyo*
PRENTICE-HALL OF SOUTHEAST ASIA PTE. LTD., *Singapore*
WHITEHALL BOOKS LIMITED, *Wellington, New Zealand*

In memory of my parents,
Sophie and Harry Rosenman

CONTENTS

Many people helped to create this book. I am deeply indebted to the individuals and couples who shared intimate details of their lives with me; to the many insightful writers who gave permission for quoting their works in this book; and to my friends, students, patients, and colleagues for their opinions and ideas. I am especially grateful to Harriet Dye for her enthusiasm, sensitivity, support in crises, and ability to clearly discern the strengths and weaknesses of the rough manuscript; to Donna McGill for her love, wisdom, perceptive comments, and faith in the project; and to Ann McMahon for her sharp mind, organizational ability, and knowledge of the English language. I would like to thank Judy Henneike, who devoted long hours to transcribing interview tapes and typing drafts of the book. I am also grateful to Joan Benedetti, Erna Bloch, Dr. Tom Hogan, Ron Hudspeth, and Melitta Inman for their special help. Finally, a grant from the Spencer Foundation provided greatly appreciated support for my research on couples with good marriages and on styles of loving.

ACKNOWLEDGMENTS

For permission to use the following material, acknowledgment is given to

Doubleday & Company for the excerpt from HOW TO TALK WITH ANYBODY ABOUT PRACTICALLY ANYTHING by Barbara Walters. Copyright © 1970 by Barbara Walters. Used by permission of Doubleday & Company, Inc.; and the excerpt from MY NEEDS, YOUR NEEDS, OUR NEEDS by Jerry Gillies. Copyright © 1974 by Jerry Gillies. Used by permission of Doubleday & Company, Inc.; and the excerpt from THE NATIONAL LOVE, SEX AND MARRIAGE TEST by Rubin Carson. Copyright © 1978 by Warren V. Bush Productions, Inc. Reprinted by permission of Doubleday & Company, Inc.

Simon & Schuster for the excerpt from *How to Win Friends and Influence People* by Dale Carnegie. Copyright ©1936 by Dale Carnegie; ©1964 by Dorothy Carnegie. Reprinted by permission of SIMON & SCHUSTER, a Division of Gulf & Western Corporation.

LOVING STYLES

Love is of all the passions the strongest,
for it attacks simultaneously the head,
the heart, and the senses.

VOLTAIRE

There is hardly any activity, any
enterprise, which is started with such
tremendous hopes and expectations and yet
which fails so regularly as love.

ERICH FROMM[1]

INTRODUCTION

Voltaire and Fromm and you would probably agree that love can be perplexing. This book, taking a new look at the intricacies of love, is designed to help you increase your ability to love and be loved.

In this scientific age, almost every segment of human behavior, including sex, is subjected to study. But many people feel that love should remain a mystery. Senator William Proxmire objected to the National Science Foundation funding a study on love. "I believe that 200 million other Americans want to leave some things in life a mystery," he insisted, "and right at the top of the things we don't want to know is why a man falls in love with a woman and vice versa. . . . Leave that to Elizabeth Barrett Browning and Irving Berlin."[2] Even Freud, who dared to probe the deepest mysteries of the human mind, confessed how little he knew about love. More recently, the American Institute for Philosophical Research concluded that the idea of love is more difficult to analyze "than the idea of freedom and much more difficult than the ideas of progress, justice and happiness."[3]

Contributing to the difficulty is our culture, which is often an obstacle to the very love it holds in such high esteem. Our society perpetuates unrealistic expectations about intimacy while providing almost no preparation for the complex task of sustaining love. The unrealistic optimism oozing out of some advertisments, songs, TV programs, and movies suggests that maintaining love requires little effort. By perpetuating false illusions and by encouraging unproductive practices, our society contributes to the problems of man–woman intimacy.

But the situation is changing. As the media become more realistic and explore formerly taboo subjects, important questions surface. Why are blissful, enduring marriages the exception? Why does the United States have the highest divorce rate in the Western world? Why are man–woman relationships so confusing, and at times, so devastating? And most important of all, why do we have so many personal, unanswered questions about love? When we are seeking the answers to these questions, the information provided by poets, novelists, and songwriters is not enough.

WHY THIS BOOK

Fortunately, research on love has become acceptable during the past decade. The new knowledge gained from this research, if put into practice, could greatly improve intimate man–woman relationships.

This book presents recent findings in practical, understandable terms. Examples, case studies, and exercises will help you to understand and to apply the latest principles for enhancing intimacy. The focus will be on man–woman intimacy, but the concepts described will often apply to other intimate relationships.

This book has evolved from my experiences as a

clinical psychologist, researcher, and teacher specializing in relationships between the sexes. In writing this book I surveyed the scientific research on love and interviewed individuals and couples who were willing to share the details of their intimate relationships. Names and specific identifying information have been changed to maintain confidentiality. These individuals, who describe their own experiences in their own words and in their own way, provide an inside look at loving.

Dr. Aubrey Richards, an anthropologist
who lived among the Bemba of northern
Rhodesia in the 1930's, once related to a
group of them an English folk tale about a
young prince who climbed glass
mountains, crossed chasms, and fought
dragons, all to obtain the hand of a
maiden he loved. The Bemba were plainly
bewildered, but remained silent. Finally an
old chief spoke up, voicing the feelings of
all present in the simplest of questions.
"Why not take another girl?" he asked.

MORTON M. HUNT[1]

STYLES
OF
LOVING

chapter one

Love means different things to different people and the words "I love you" have special individual meaning. Perhaps some of our difficulty with the concept of love has to do with the fact that the single word *love* bears the impossible burden of defining an idea so complex and so multifaceted that it defies a single definition. Usually, a society develops many words for categorizing an important occurrence. For example, an Eskimo has seventeen different ways to describe and differentiate types of snow. In a society such as ours, where love assumes so much importance, part of the difficulty with understanding the concept is that the single word is inadequate to describe the complexities and kinds of loving.

Recent research indicates that there are six main styles of loving. This chapter combines the work of three sociologists—John Alan Lee, Tom Lasswell, and Marcia Lasswell, with my own research, and explores the implications of these styles of loving. The six basic lovestyles are: Friendship, Giving, Possessive, Practical, Game-Playing, and Erotic.

You can determine your own concept of love by taking the fifty-item test near the end of this chapter. Scoring the test shows you your position on each of the six lovestyles. If you would like to take the test before reading the chapter, turn to page 24.

When reading the description for each style of loving, bear in mind that a person can score high in more than one lovestyle. The test, providing an overall profile, shows the extent to which a person conforms to each of the six styles of loving.

FRIENDSHIP LOVE

Sharing, mutual understanding, respect, compassion, and concern characterize friendship lovers. As good friends, they feel comfortable with each other and assume that their relationship will be permanent. They enjoy the security, the naturalness, the comfortableness of their love.

Friendship love usually develops gradually. Sexual intimacy often comes late in the relationship, emerging from the already existing verbal intimacy. And many friendship lovers do not realize they are in love until they have been for some time.

This lovestyle shows less preoccupation with the beloved than do the other lovestyles. Mostly absent are intense emotions, either painful or ecstatic. Taking a less romantic attitude, the intimates may forget or minimize the importance of birthdays, anniversaries, and other significant occasions.

Friendship lovers

> never spend much time looking into each other's eyes or talking about their love for each other. Such behavior would seem ridiculous to them. Perhaps neither will be

able to recall when "I love you" was first said, if indeed any special declaration of love was ever made. Not that they deliberately avoid such statements; more likely they simply reserve them for very special situations, such as the eve of a long separation. After all, how often do you say to a close friend, "I am your close friend"?[2]

Stability, rather than impulsiveness, permeates the relationship—the comfort of the home environment, the power of patience and loyalty, the endurance of brother–sister type love. Even if these lovers break up or move on, they try to maintain contact, and they usually have good friendships with their former intimates. This lovestyle is supportive and undemanding, allowing each partner time to pursue hobbies, platonic friendships, and professional interests. With the passage of time, shared and discussed activities enhance mutual understanding and the friendship grows.

Arthur and Linda, friendship lovers, have been married for sixteen years. Linda says:

> We can talk all night and all day. We can't find enough time to talk about things. Whatever we're into, we study it and really get into it deeply. We also devote a lot of time to talking about the department he manages at work. I know the quirks of all the people in it. Arthur uses me as a sounding board and wants my opinion. He also wants to know about our children. When I'm around, he'll talk to me rather than do his work at home.
>
> I think we're very well matched. We both took a monogamous relationship for granted, and we are totally committed to our marriage. I just feel like we'll be together until our eighties, and we'll be talking until the other one takes a last breath. I just can't imagine life without him. We have all that shared history.

Pitfalls. Some observers would find the predictability, security, stability, and quiet homelife of this type of love to be lacking in excitement. Compared to the possessive, game-playing, and erotic types of love, friendship love is uneventful. "Arthur is like the rock of ages," says Linda. "You can set your watch by his jogging on Monday, Wednesday, and Friday. I know I can depend on him, and his predictability gives me a sense of stability. I also know I'm responsible for adding some variety to our relationship." Arthur and Linda have a good marriage. And by realizing the need for variety, Linda avoids a problem faced by some friendship relationships—the pitfall of drifting into a dull routine.

In the following excerpt from Somerset Maugham's *Of Human Bondage,* Sally, an extreme friendship lover, does not allow a marriage proposal to interfere with her routine.

"I wonder if you'll marry me, Sally . . ."

"If you like."

"Don't you want to?"

"Oh, of course I'd like to have a house of my own and it's about time I was settling down . . ."

"But don't you want to marry me?"

"There's no one else I would marry."

"Then that settles it."

"Mother and dad will be surprised, won't they?"

"I'm so happy."

"I want my lunch," she said.[3]

GIVING LOVE

As the name implies, giving lovers are giving and forgiving. Placing the happiness and best interests of their intimates ahead of their own, they are patient, understanding, and supportive. They have a sense of duty and obligation not only to the beloved but also to other people and to society in general. They are dependable and will come through in a crisis. Giving lovers are compassionate, altruistic, committed, loyal, and patient.

Like friendship lovers, giving lovers gradually develop, rather than fall into, love. They seek an ideal love relationship rather than an ideal type of person. Giving lovers try to perceive and accept the needs of the intimate and derive more pleasure from giving than from receiving. They have the ability to allow the partner to do what he/she needs to do and will go so far as to tolerate the partner's participation in activities that are incompatible with their own values. The giving lover will even consider giving up the intimate if that will be to the intimate's benefit, even though there will be personal pain felt as a result of the loss. The giving lover does not want to stand in the intimate's way and understands the old saying that "it is better to have loved and lost than never to have loved at all."

Giving lovers respect and value love. Like great artists, they strive for perfect expression that transcends self.

The giving lover is committed to the relationship, and is not deterred by everyday annoyances. A 30-year-old woman with a 5-year-old daughter from her first marriage speaks about her new husband:

> If I'm bitchy he takes it and is still loving. Sometimes I feel he loves me more when I'm mean. When my mood is over he says he doesn't mind the bitchiness because I'm so nice other times. . . .
>
> He also feels that giving love to his new daughter is important even though she sometimes doesn't respond well to him. She hurts him very much because she has not accepted him as number one daddy while he has done so much to show that he loves her.

Pitfalls: The 26-year-old girlfriend of a giving lover says:

> If I said I wanted something it appeared. Ralph made an effort to get whatever I wanted. I never wanted to say what I needed because it might be beyond his financial means or it might seem as if I was asking for something. I recall one night saying I was out of tea. The next morning there was a box of tea bags taped to the steering wheel of my car.
>
> The first time Ralph gave me something it was dear. But it got most annoying after a while. You get tired of the giving because it's out of balance. It's not special if it's done all the time. It's like someone who tells you fifty times a day that he loves you.

Unlike Ralph, few giving lovers inundate their intimates with material possessions, but the example does illustrate how too much giving of any kind can become irritating rather than special. A relationship is likely to become boring if one partner excessively puts the needs and wants of the other ahead of his/her own. This is especially true in the sexual area, where at least some self-interest is needed. If one partner is so concerned with giving that she/ he becomes a spectator rather than a true participant, sex can lose its excitement.

POSSESSIVE LOVE

Possessive lovers view jealousy as an integral part of being in love, and make statements such as "I am jealous because I love you so much" or "If you loved me, you would be more jealous." Obsessed with love, they require attention and affection and togetherness.

Possessive love

is the theme of innumerable romantic novels. Its familiar
characteristics—extreme jealousy, helpless obsession, and
a tragic ending—are used in literature to create human
conflict and portray noble self-sacrifice. The [possessive]
lover is a writer's delight because he is full of paradoxes.
Having found the one true love in life, he is unable to
relax and enjoy it, but instead becomes gripped by fear of
losing the beloved. His love relationship, far from sup-
porting and fulfilling his other roles in life, begins to
subvert and consume every portion of his activity. He is
wracked by yearning and moodiness. He alternates between momentary highs of irrational joy and depressing
downers of loneliness whenever the beloved is absent or
angry. He knows his insufferable possessiveness defeats
his own cause but he can't help feeling it—and worse—
showing it.[4]

The possessive lover requires much time with his
intimate and cannot tolerate times apart. Even brief separations elicit frequent phone calls. Sheila, the ex-girlfriend
of a possessive lover, recalls "how frequently he used the
telephone to check my whereabouts. I can vividly remember
being paged at the local grocery store in order to make sure
I got there safely and to add Oreos to my shopping list."

Preoccupied with thoughts of the intimate, the possessive lover showers him/her with attention. Operating on
the assumption that true love is not easy, he is upset over
little slights, is elated by dramatic moments of coming
together, and has a need to create problems when none
exist. The possessive lover feels that this important love
must be constantly tested, and emotional agitation is a
small price to pay when experiencing deep love.

Pitfalls. Although many people like to possess an intimate completely, or feel security in being possessed, the jealousy, clinging, and forced togetherness of possessive love inevitably create problems. A possessive lover will eventually become burdensome to a more self-sufficient partner.

"He wanted to be my sole source of happiness and he tried to isolate me from my family and friends," complained Sheila. She continued:

> As an example, my mother, who lived in another state, took a bad fall and sprained her leg. Immediately I scheduled emergency annual leave from my job. When I told my boyfriend about this emergency, he got very upset since I did not include him in my plans, and thought we should have made a vacation out of this trip, since my mother lived in Florida. He did not understand why I had to make this trip alone, and he felt I was purposely excluding him. His final overall response to this situation was, "Without me, you're not going to have fun anyway." He never forgave me for making this trip by myself and tried very hard to make me feel guilty for leaving him behind.
>
> Soon after my mother's recovery, she paid me a visit, as she frequently did, three or four times a year. My boyfriend, who was extremely jealous of my mother, welcomed her with open arms for the first few days of her visit. Knowing that her visit with me would last a week, he took it upon himself to check the airline schedules for earlier flights for her return home. Then he immediately started talking her into rescheduling her original flight and actually convinced her to leave two days early. Before I realized what was happening, my mother was safely home in Florida, with thoughts that she was imposing on our relationship.

Practical lovers plan their lives, relying more on logical thoughts than on feelings. They realistically evaluate their own assets, appraise their "market value," and try to obtain the best possible deal in a partner. The practical lover, when involved with the right person, will be dependable and loving and will be committed to the mutual solution of any problems that might arise. In Lee's words,

> A pragmatic choice in lovestyles might seem rather calculating, and most of us are likely to make our approach a little less obvious by avoiding written lists. We keep our lists in our heads because popular literature and social values about love often persuade us that we should be romantic rather than levelheaded about love. We tend to ridicule those who are too practical in their choice of mate, as in this old joke: WIFE WANTED: Frontier farmer, steady, hardworking, good provider, seeks levelheaded wife who is sober, strong, and owns a late-model tractor ... send picture of tractor.[5]

In a sense, this is shopping-list love; the person decides what particular assets he or she wants and then attempts to find a suitable partner. Practical lovers discuss their future aspirations and help each other to achieve the sought-after goals. Practical lovers choose a partner for their planned lifestyle, commit themselves to finding a common-sense, practical solution to everyday problems, and accept a less idealistic view of love with fewer unrealistic expectations. Not surprisingly, they usually have stable relationships.

A practical lover will not select a mate who deviates too far from the ideal pattern, as the following example of

Gloria illustrates. Gloria, a strikingly attractive second-year medical student, is divorced and the mother of two children. She reflected,

> To survive, I need to be practical, but at times I feel I may be too calculating. Doug wants to marry me and in many ways I love him. He's intelligent and considerate, we have a great sex life, and my two sons get along well with him. But I've decided not to marry him. He's in the army, and he's going to be transferred in a few months. He will probably get transferred every three years. I want to stay in the same place and be able to establish a stable medical practice. Ideally, I would like to get involved with an older physician, who would love me and my sons, and who would help me get established in practice. I think I have a good chance of meeting this type person at medical conferences.

Realistically, considering the assets Gloria possesses, her chances of meeting her ideal person are good. Like most practical lovers, she wants to have a satisfying love relationship which will be compatible with her pre-established life plan.

Pitfalls. Problems will occur if one of the partners can no longer meet the needs of the other, or if one partner decides to pursue different life objectives which are unacceptable to the other. Practical lovers will at first attempt to find a rational solution to the incompatibility and will often consider professional help. If they cannot come up with an acceptable solution, they may plan a separation or a divorce based upon practical considerations—such as when the partner completes college or when a certain goal is reached or when the children grow older.

Game-playing lovers try to minimize dependency and commitment. The game, when properly played, controls involvement and prevents the participants from being hurt. Partners best suited for this lovestyle are undemanding and self-sufficient. Love, like a well, is viewed as a good thing to drink from, but a bad thing to fall into.[6]

By having two or more partners at the same time, the game-playing lover can lessen commitment, increase excitement, and have someone in reserve so that he or she can quickly move on if problems arise. Variety and good times are the goal, and as much emphasis is placed on playing the game as on winning the prize. For Barry, the excitement comes from playing the moves that have to be played to get the relationship to a certain point.

> I get bored pretty quickly with a one-to-one relationship. I keep multiple relationships to maintain the excitement and to avoid being hurt. And I try to keep the women I'm dating unaware of my other escapades. I'll give you an example of one of my techniques. I have developed a cassette tape which has out-of-town telephone noises on it, so I can call someone and pretend to be out-of-town. It's an excellent way to lead a second life, a third life . . .

Placing emphasis on quantity, game-players are good at meeting people and are not too selective in their choice of partners. The philosophy is that if you're not with the one you love, then love the one you're with. Love is a game with much fun while it lasts.

Game-players thrive on excitement and challenge.

And like tennis players, equally matched partners have the most interesting games. Bill, a confirmed game-player, says:

> The longest relationship I've ever had was with another game-playing lover. We had been living together for eight months when one night she came over to me with a very serious look on her face and began crying. She can really put on the tears when she wants to. And with more tears, she sobs, "Bill, I have a confession; I have been sleeping with someone other than you for the past month." This really relieved a lot of my guilt since I had been sleeping with two other women. I held her and said, "Sweetheart, don't worry about it; I still care for you. Everything's fine." In the meantime, inside I'm still going WHEW, one less thing I have to worry about. But she kept crying and feeling bad. Finally I did the only thing I could do to make her feel better. I said, "Joan, don't feel bad, I've had one too." And all of a sudden the crying stops and a big smile comes on her face and she says, "Ah-hah! I knew it—I knew it! I haven't been sleeping with anyone else. But I knew that was the only way I was going to get it out of you."
>
> Then we both had the desire to make love, because it intensified the game, the excitement.

Pitfalls. Although game-playing lovers try to avoid involvement and commitment, one partner may lose the feeling of detachment and fall into the well. Becoming overly involved is likely to result in problems. The game is no longer fun, and unless both participants are willing to modify the rules, the game is abruptly terminated. A particularly awkward, though not infrequent, situation occurs when one partner is a possessive lover.

Game-players, at times, feel guilty about their lovestyle. Many of them view game-playing as a fun stage to pass through, rather than as a permanent lifestyle.

EROTIC LOVE

Erotic lovers search for their preconceived physical ideal. They emphasize quality rather than quantity, believe in the possibility of love at first sight, and become excited and energized when they finally find love. The closer the partner comes to the ideal—body build, face, hair, height, skin, fragrance, voice, intellect, personality—the more the enchantment.

Sex and deep personal sharing usually come early because once the potential ideal person appears, the erotic lover wants to plunge into the relationship. John Alan Lee says,

> Sexual knowledge is profoundly related to personal knowledge on a wider basis. Much that the erotic lover comes to know about his or her beloved during the first stage of the relationship occurs simultaneously with, or as a product of, sensual enjoyment and genital contact. A successful erotic approach to love must include a willingness to reveal yourself to your partner openly and unashamedly, to express your feelings with great honesty, and to elicit a similar response from your partner. In time, this personal rapport cements the relationship after the original physical intensity has leveled off.[7]

Commitment at first is intense, with a desire to discuss experiences ranging from day-to-day activities to past lovers to childhood memories. Erotic lovers enter into a monogamous relationship, experiment with sexual techniques, and search for new ways to please each other. Erotic love, like a fire on which most of the available logs have been piled, burns at first with great intensity—but like the fire, the intensity is destined to diminish.

The erotic relationship between Herb and Wendy points out some of the pleasures and pitfalls of erotic love. One Friday night at a large party, Herb and Wendy met and experienced powerful erotic attraction. "Over a hundred people were roving around the house, but we were so into each other that it was like nobody else was there." They spent the night together and did not separate for two days. By the end of the weekend they knew they were made for each other.

Herb had felt instant attraction for Wendy. "Her hair really turned me on; I saw sensuality in her eyes; and I liked the foxy way she dressed, and her very nice breasts." Throughout the weekend, the sharing of deep feelings and experiences accompanied the intense physical attraction. After the weekend, Herb thought, "Here is a woman both attractive and independent with a sensuality to match my own."

"When I saw him, I was very physically attracted," Wendy said. "I liked the black beard, the black curly hair, and the beautiful blue eyes. His look was very sexy—the open shirt, his necklace, and the tight pants he had on. We had a fantastic weekend together, and I thought that not only was he physically attractive, but he seemed like the type man who really knew how to take care of a woman." The sensual massage which Herb gave her before lovemaking Sunday afternoon reaffirmed Wendy's intense feelings. "Monday I walked into work and said I'd met the guy I was going to marry." Three months later, Herb and Wendy married.

Pitfalls. A year after that, they came in for marriage counseling, feeling disappointed and disillusioned. Wendy had projected her ideal onto Herb, and Herb had projected his ideal onto her. Not surprisingly, erotic lovers, driven by their strong desire to find the ideal mate, assume that their intimates have characteristics which they simply do not possess. Putting one's best foot forward and assuming what one wants to assume can at first maintain the illusion, but life on a day-to-day basis eventually shatters the perceived ideal.

Erotic love, with its intensity of emotions, has many peaks and valleys. The powerful attraction of the first several weeks provides the exhilaration of being on a high mountain, but coming down is inevitable. Successful erotic lovers appreciate what they have and are willing to settle for less than the highest peak. Other erotic lovers, unable to sustain the initial excitement and unwilling to tolerate lower levels of passion, move on and often enter into a series of intense monogamous relationships.

But repeaters in erotic love must be willing to accept often long periods between erotic relationships, because the specific type of lover they seek is hard to find. Perhaps partly for the same reason, erotic lovers may face much hurt if they attempt to have playful short-term relationships with partners too close to their ideal. If the partner is near the ideal, avoiding overinvolvement will be difficult.

STYLES OF LOVING CAN CHANGE

Unlike an astrological sign, a person's style of loving can change. An individual's lovestyle is influenced by experiences and by evolving wants and needs. Moreover, different relationships may bring out or may subdue different styles of loving. Often one partner will influence the other partner's lovestyle, resulting in a more compatible combination. This is illustrated in the following account written by a college senior.

I am 21 years old, intelligent, popular, and quite handsome according to many women. Because of the above reasons and more, I have been spoiled by the female sex. I have never had any problems being successful with women. I have done almost anything that I have wanted to almost anyone that I chose to do it to. I have taken women and used them until I no longer found them fun.

Having been trusted and doing so much wrong, I had decided that "what goes around, comes around," and I was going to make certain that I never trusted anyone to the extent that they were able to do to me what I had done to others.

Six months ago I took the "styles of loving" test. The test revealed me as a game-player. Basing my answers on my most recent relationship at that time, I most certainly was. My lowest score was as a giver in a relationship, and this too was highly accurate and descriptive of me. In my opinion, the test projected the real me, not only as I saw myself, but also as I really was. I say "was," because I am different now, and if I took the test again, I would obtain different scores.

Now, I have met a young lady who is very beautiful, intelligent, popular; like me, she is capable of breaking many hearts. She seems to be everything that I have looked for in a woman; anything I have ever dreamed of in a future wife, she is. I have always been told that one day the lady that I really fall in love with will be the one to turn the tables on me and retaliate for all those I've played with.

I am quite aware that she can hurt me, because I have let

my guard down for the first time. I have always looked at relationships in a playful manner, often comparing myself and a woman to two fighters. Both of us are capable of delivering blows of intimate and intense love that would cause the other to "submit" and fall in love. Though I always passed some of the most devastating and dazzling blows to my "opponent," I have always been able to keep my guard up, preventing myself from receiving that which could possibly cause me to "fall."

As I enter into this match for the next round, I am about prepared to drop my defenses enough to receive some of the blows from this impressive young opponent. I know that she is able to penetrate the least drop in my guard. I also know that I could receive permanent damage from the blows, but I have all but decided to fall in love. I actually trust this woman, even though I know that she could be the one to hurt me as I have done others. I have been playing games for a long time. Now, I'm ready to fall in love, and I wonder if I am setting myself up for hurt. If so, chalk up one to experience, because I am falling.

A few months ago, I looked at myself and asked, "Do you want to be a game-player forever?" I knew that I did not; I've always wanted concrete and sure things in my life. Born under the sign of Taurus, I'm determined to achieve, but we all need solid foundations to build on.

This lady walked into my life at a time when I was ready to receive the love that she had to offer. There's no real event that caused me to seek true love and it really developed because I had to decide that I am mature enough to be real and love someone genuinely. This lady simply arrived at a most appropriate time. Somehow she must have seen the need that I have for love, and obviously she feels qualified to fulfill the requirements.

So, these feelings developed because I have become more intimate and honest with myself; therefore, I feel more apt to be honest and intimate with others, especially this particular woman. Perhaps she does not feel the same.

She could be a game-player who is only in it for fun as I often was. It could be true that she has heard of my past relationships and is out to try and be the first to cause me to fall. Regardless, I am now ready to trust and to develop a very intimate relationship. My guard is down. Will I be defeated?

Three months later, this student and his girlfriend made plans to get married.

Although an individual's style of loving can change, many couples will follow a relatively consistent lovestyle throughout life.

COMPATIBLE COMBINATIONS

In general, intimates with the same style of loving are compatible. An exception might be possessive lovers who, propelled by jealousy and restrained by holding on too tightly, have a roller-coaster type of relationship. The most stable and enduring relationships occur between friendship lovers, between giving lovers, and between practical lovers, in the above order. Game-players get along best with other game-players, but the emphasis is on fun together while it lasts, rather than on making future plans. Erotics, despite the ecstasy of the first few months, will fare best if they accept the inevitable lessening of the romance and if they supplement their erotic style with an additional lovestyle.

Intimates with different lovestyles can also form compatible combinations. The possibilities are listed below:

Friendship —with Giving or Practical

Giving—with all types except Game-Playing

Possessive—with Giving, and under the right circumstances with Practical or Erotic, or to a lesser extent with Friendship

Practical—with Giving or Friendship and, under the right circumstances, with all the other types

Game-playing—best with Game-Playing, but under the right circumstances with Practical

Erotic—under the right circumstances with Friendship, Giving, Practical, or Possessive, if that person meets erotic ideals

When analyzing compatibilities, remember that a person's pattern in all six of the lovestyles has great importance. To look only at the highest score would be oversimplifying the complicated way in which a person loves.

THE STYLES OF LOVING
TEST*

In responding to the items below, when it is appropriate think of your most significant peer love relationships. If you cannot decide which has been the most significant, think of your most recent significant love relationship. If you wish you may think of your ideal love relationship whether you have actually experienced it or not. Answer *all* of the following items either true or false.

1. I believe that "love at first sight" is possible.
2. I did not realize that I was in love until I actually had been for some time.

---

* Thomas E. Lasswell and Marcia E. Lasswell, "I Love You But I'm Not In Love With You," *Journal of Marriage and Family Counseling,* 2, no. 3 (1976), 222–24. Used with permission.

3. When things aren't going right with us, my stomach gets upset.

4. From a practical point of view, I must consider what a person is going to become in life before I commit myself to loving him/her.

5. You cannot have love unless you have first had *caring* for a while.

6. It's always a good idea to keep your lover a little uncertain about how committed you are to him/her.

7. The first time we kissed or rubbed cheeks, I felt a definite genital response (lubrication, erection).

8. I still have good friendships with almost everyone with whom I have ever been involved in a love relationship.

9. It makes good sense to plan your life carefully before you choose a lover.

10. When my love affairs break up, I get so depressed that I have even thought of suicide.

11. Sometimes I get so excited about being in love that I can't sleep.

12. I try to use my own strength to help my lover through difficult times, even when he/she is behaving foolishly.

13. I would rather suffer myself than let my lover suffer.

14. Part of the fun of being in love is testing one's skill at keeping it going and getting what one wants from it at the same time.

15. As far as my lovers go, what they don't know about me doesn't hurt them.

16. It is best to love someone with a similar background.

17. We kissed each other soon after we met because we both wanted to.

18. When my lover doesn't pay attention to me, I feel sick all over.

19. I cannot be happy unless I place my lover's happiness before my own.

20. Usually the first thing that attracts my attention to a person is his/her pleasing physical appearance.

21. The best kind of love grows out of a long friendship.

22. When I am in love, I have trouble concentrating on anything else.

23. At the first touch of his/her hand, I knew that love was a real possibility.

24. When I break up with someone, I go out of my way to see that he/she is O.K.

25. I cannot relax if I suspect that he/she is with someone else.

26. I have at least once had to plan carefully to keep two of my lovers from finding out about each other.

27. I can get over love affairs pretty easily and quickly.

28. A main consideration in choosing a lover is how he/she reflects on my family.

29. The best part of love is living together, building a home together, and rearing children together.

30. I am usually willing to sacrifice my own wishes to let my lover achieve his/hers.

31. A main consideration in choosing a partner is whether or not he/she will be a good parent.

32. Kissing, cuddling, and sex shouldn't be rushed into; they will happen naturally when one's intimacy has grown enough.

33. I enjoy flirting with attractive people.

34. My lover would get upset if she/he knew some of the things I've done with other people.

35. Before I ever fell in love, I had a pretty clear physical picture of what my true love would be like.

36. If my lover had a baby by someone else, I would want to raise it, love it, and care for it as if it were my own.

37. It is hard to say exactly when we fell in love.

38. I couldn't truly love anyone I would not be willing to marry.

39. Even though I don't want to be jealous, I can't help it when he/she pays attention to someone else.

40. I would rather break up with my lover than to stand in his/her way.

41. I like the idea of me and my lover having the same kinds of clothes, hats, plants, bicycles, cars, etc.

42. I wouldn't date anyone that I wouldn't want to fall in love with.

43. At least once when I thought a love affair was all over, I saw him/her again and knew I couldn't realistically see him/her without loving him/her.

44. Whatever I own is my lover's to use as he/she chooses.

45. If my lover ignores me for a while, I sometimes do really stupid things to try to get his/her attention back.

46. It's fun to see whether I can get someone to go out with me even if I don't want to get involved with that person.

47. A main consideration in choosing a mate is how he/she will reflect on one's career.

48. When my lover doesn't see me or call for a while, I assume he/she has a good reason.

49. Before getting very involved with anyone, I try to figure out how compatible his/ her hereditary background is with mine in case we ever have children.

50. The best love relationships are the ones that last the longest.

SCORING

Score only your "True" answers.

Your friendship love score is the number of "True" answers to questions 2, 5, 8, 21, 29, 32, 37, 50.

Your giving love score is the number of "True" answers to questions 12, 13, 19, 24, 30, 36, 40, 44, 48.

Your possessive love score is the number of "True" answers to questions 3, 10, 11, 18, 22, 25, 39, 43, 45.

Your practical love score is the number of "True" answers to questions 4, 9, 16, 28, 31, 38, 42, 47, 49.

Your game-playing love score is the number of "True" answers to questions 6, 14, 15, 26, 27, 33, 34, 46.

Your erotic love score is the number of "True" answers to questions 1, 7, 17, 20, 23, 35, 41.

	Love Score	*Percentile*
Friendship	_____	_____
Giving	_____	_____
Possessive	_____	_____
Practical	_____	_____
Game-Playing	_____	_____
Erotic	_____	_____

To get the correct percentile, use the table on page 29 for each love score.

PERCENTILES FOR EACH OF THE STYLES OF LOVING

		Friend-ship	Giving	Possessive	Practical	Game-Playing	Erotic
	0	1	1	3	4	1	1
	1	5	2	11	12	6	2
	2	16	8	28	26	14	29
	3	33	25	38	48	26	52
LOVE	4	56	47	53	70	34	74
SCORE	5	78	56	64	83	59	91
	6	88	71	80	91	80	98
	7	95	91	91	97	95	99
	8	99	97	96	99	99	
	9		99	99			

INTERPRETING THE TEST

Your percentile score for each style of loving tells you how you compare with other people who have taken the test. In other words, a percentile score of 78 on a lovestyle would indicate that you were higher on that lovestyle than 78 percent of the people. A percentile score of 50 on another scale would place you in the middle. A percentile score of 5 would indicate that 95 percent of the people were higher than you on that scale.

As mentioned earlier, different relationships bring out different lovestyles. You might be interested in retaking the test using a different relationship as the basis.

*To love one's self is the beginning
of a life-long romance.*

OSCAR WILDE[1]

BECOMING
INTIMATE
WITH
YOURSELF

chapter two

31

Self-acceptance provides a firm foundation for building love. All too often, relationships fail because one or both of the partners believes that he or she is not worthy of being loved. Although an intimate relationship can contribute to self-acceptance and self-esteem, a feeling that one is worthy of love is usually a prerequisite. The situation is analogous to that of the individual who states, "I wouldn't join any club that has low enough standards to invite me to join." Feelings of unworthiness and unlovableness often defeat a relationship before it begins.

Without self-acceptance, happiness will be elusive. Happiness comes from within, and the belief that another person can make us happy is an illusion. "We tell ourselves," writes Ken Keyes, "if only I could find the right person to love, then I would be happy. So we search for someone who our addictions tell us is the right person—and we experience some pleasurable moments. But since we don't know how to love, the relationship gradually deteriorates. Then we decide we didn't have the right person after all! As we grow into higher consciousness, we discover that it is more important to be the right person than to find the right person."[2]

Being the right person involves knowing yourself.

Socrates' simple admonition "Know thyself" provides a path for achieving the good life, but it is more difficult than it sounds. To know yourself fully, you have to face yourself honestly, looking through facades, shams, and pretenses. You have to reconcile discrepancies between saying and doing and discrepancies between accomplishments and hopes. You have to accept a simple psychological truth: You create, rather than find, your self.

> Attaining a healthy self-image with its concomitant feelings of adequacy, ableness, personal worth, and confidence is not some lofty goal beyond mortal reach, standing as a kind of poetic ideal. It is an attitude or cluster of attitudes that are learned and acquired, which means that sometimes "bad" (negative, destructive, self-defeating) attitudes must be replaced by healthier attitudes. Most people seem to want to move forward toward higher levels of physical and psychological health, although we would have to admit that there are those odd personalities who seem to get a perverse pleasure out of *un*health and suffering because it is the chief way of knowing they're alive. Sometimes we hear people say they would like to change their neurotic ways and have healthier attitudes about themselves and others, but then say they can't change because, after all, their unfortunate childhood experiences made them the way they are. So busy are they blaming the past, contriving new defenses, inventing new excuses, and enjoying their own self-pity that they seldom have any energy left over for considering more constructive avenues for living and looking ahead to better days.[3]

Some people dwell on past defeats and cling to suffering because it gives them a sense of understanding and predictability in an otherwise complicated world. They find security in repeating past mistakes and in avoiding new ways of relating. They fear change and justify inaction with statements such as "I've always been this way," and "I am this way because of my past experiences." Old ways of behaving are comfortable; new ways of behaving involve risk and work. Some people wallow in past misfortunes, dislike themselves, and ignore opportunities for change and growth.

Other individuals, as Ron Hudspeth illustrates in his newspaper column, overcome past handicaps and do not allow experiences of rejection to undermine self-confidence permanently.

"It was," says Sybil without hesitation, "the greatest evening of my life."

I should describe Sybil to you.

She is a pretty Atlanta brunette in her late 20s. She has curves in the right spots. Guys' heads turn when she passes.

But Sybil is far from all body and no brains. She is single, one day will have her PhD, and is financially—and otherwise—independent. . . .

Let us zip back more than 10 years and meet Sybil, 16-year-old student at a Tennessee high school.

Say hello to the ugly duckling. Make that fat ugly duckling. Sybil weighed 185 pounds.

"I had exactly one date in four years of high school," she recalls, "and it was with a boy everyone else in school made fun of. Even he didn't ask me out again."

Sybil was never invited to parties. She missed the prom. The crowning blow came when they borrowed Sybil's convertible to parade the homecoming queen. "That," says Sybil "makes you feel rotten."

If that wasn't enough social stigma to bear growing up in the fragile '50s, Sybil had another burden—she was intelligent.

"I was known as the fat and smart kid," she recalls. "I got to be part of all the organizations that had nothing to do with social acceptance—student council, stage manager for the play, Junior Red Cross, first aid room attendant."

Once the star of the football team walked up and smiled at Sybil. She nearly melted. "Will you do my homework?" he asked, tossed her his notebook, and walked off.

"That was the only time he ever spoke to me," said Sybil. "As I look back, kids in the '50s were probably the cruelest of all. If you weren't a part of the 'in' crowd, you were made to feel awful. Thankfully, teenagers aren't that way today."

One day not long ago, Sybil was thumbing through some old mail. She came across an invitation to her 10-year class reunion.

She ripped it open and discovered the deadline for accepting was that day. It was being organized by a girl who had been Miss Everything in the class of '66.

Sybil called and told her who she was.

"Oh," said Miss Everything, disinterested. "I think you might be too late."

Sybil wasn't about to miss the reunion. "I wasn't going to take 'no' for an answer," she smiled. "I told her one more plate couldn't matter, and if it did, well, I just wouldn't eat."

"Well, okay," said Miss Everything, "I guess it's okay if you come."

The reunion couldn't have come at a better time for Sybil. She was the slimmest she'd ever been in her life. She was beautifully tanned, which accented a low-cut dress "that was so sensuous and tasteful at the same time that it frightened me when I saw myself in the mirror. I couldn't believe it was me. I really think I could have been on the cover of Cosmopolitan."

She arrived at the reunion party alone, nervous about only one inevitable happening—the first meeting in 10 years with Paul.

"Paul had lived across the street from me," said Sybil, "and I'd always had a mad crush on him. But I was so shy I'd never talked to him. He was always dating the beautiful girls anyway."

When Sybil walked in the door, heads turned and conversation faded to a hush.

"One girl just stood there and looked at me with her mouth open," said Sybil. "Another one—who had ignored me in school—finally walked up and said, 'How are you? You can't be Sybil.' "

All eyes followed Sybil as she made her way across a room filled with old classmates. It was at that moment that her eyes meet Paul's.

"Sybil!" he shouted across the room. "I thought that was you. You are absolutely beautiful."

"I don't think I've ever had a better moment in my life," recalls Sybil. "I had to contain myself to keep from getting tacky. I kept thinking over and over, 'here you are— Fat Sybil— knocking 'em dead.' "

Paul insisted on sitting by her at dinner. Guys lined up to dance with her. The football captain who had asked her to do his homework came to Atlanta to see her.

She danced with every guy there until the reunion moved into the wee hours.

As she was about to leave, she bumped into two red-headed sisters who had been part of the "in" crowd. "I remembered because I'd had to sell the Key Club calendar with their photos in it," said Sybil. "They never spoke to me."

The two sisters had avoided Sybil the entire evening, but could no longer contain their emotions.

"I wish," said one of the sisters, "I could trade places with you. You have a career, you live in an exciting city and there must be lots of men . . . Your life is like something out of a magazine."

"It isn't, of course," said Sybil, "but I wasn't about to tell her differently. If there was ever one moment at the party, that I was maybe guilty of being cruel, this was it."

The night ended and Paul walked her to her car and kissed her goodnight.

"It was like a movie fade-out," recalls Sybil. "The last thing I remember was looking back as I drove off and seeing one of the red-headed girls sitting on the steps all alone with her head buried in her hands."

"It was like she was saying: 'It was supposed to be my night. What happened?' But I'll tell you whose night it was. It was a night for everyone who ever had a handicap as a teenager, for anyone who had ever been treated cruelly. It was a triumph for little people." [4]

Sybil couldn't change the past, but she did magnificently transcend the limiting labels of her teenage years. She decided what she wanted, took the initiative, and determined her lifestyle. She created the self that she wanted.

Most of us will not change as visibly as Sybil did, and we may not have an opportunity like Sybil's reunion to re-enter a past experience in a new way. More subtle changes may also make big differences in a person's lifestyle. Amy, for example, came for therapy after ten years of a fairly good marriage. She liked her husband and three children, but felt ill at ease and vaguely unhappy. By exploring her past and her own thoughts, she made an important discovery:

All the women in my family—mother, grandmother, aunts—seemed to exist for giving. They gave and gave, and it often made me feel bad because the other side of the coin was that they made you feel guilty if you didn't appreciate what they gave. They did the martyr thing.

I guess I've always had the feeling I didn't want to be that way, but at the same time I thought that, as a wife and mother, I was supposed to give, give, give—no choice. It seems like I nearly lost the ability to decide what *I* wanted since I thought everybody else's wants came first.

Since I've realized that, I've been changing. And my whole outlook has changed since I've discovered I can choose what I want to do, depending on how I feel about a situation. I like choosing; funny thing is I think my family likes me better, now, too.

As Amy discovered, the habits and patterns learned in childhood are often subtle and strong. Sometimes work and exploration are necessary before the old can be routed and the new built in. Most importantly, Amy and Sybil and others like them have realized that they can come to grips with the past, that they can make their own choices, and that they can determine their own actions.

When people take charge of their lives, they multiply their possibilities for realizing hopes and dreams. This leads to another psychological truth: You have more control over what happens in your life than you realize.

TAKING CHARGE OF YOUR LIFE

Taking more control of your life makes you more the master of your fate, and encourages you to accept more responsibility for what happens. Blaming other people or using the excuse of bad luck to justify failures becomes harder; programming yourself for more self-confidence and for more success becomes easier. You create a better life for yourself as you increase self-confidence, positive thinking, and concentration. You also become more aware of your own actions.

Observing your own actions can give you important clues about hidden feelings. Virginia, a graduate student, observed that every time she had a date she would spend the days beforehand fretting about what clothes to wear. She began to realize that she felt very unsure of herself, and that her feelings were surfacing in her excessive worry about what she should wear on a date. She began to focus upon feeling better about herself, and her anxiety about what to wear soon disappeared. Like Virginia, most of us express our feelings of insecurity in excessive concerns about something which, under other circumstances, might seem inconsequential. You can learn much about your own feelings by looking for those areas of your life where you show excessive upset, worry, or concern.

Making your own choices, although at times difficult, increases your potential for self-discovery and self-actualization. If you want to become all you are capable of becoming, use your feelings, your intuition, and your intelligence for reaching decisions. To tap your potential you have to look within, and you have to decide what will make you feel good about yourself.

People who clearly decide what they want are more likely to achieve their objectives. Yet many people have only vague goals and values. In the exercise that follows, you will probably find that the individuals you most admire have definite goals.

Take some time to think of the five people you admire most. These people need not be living today. They can be historical figures, they can be famous people, they can be individuals you personally know. List their names in the space below, and next to each, in a few words, write what you admire most about that person.

1. _____

2. _____

3. _____

4. _____

5. _____

Chances are that many of the traits these people possess are characteristics you yourself would like to have. Think about what type life you want for yourself. What are your goals and values? And what have you done to achieve your goals?

Now think about what you do well, about what you are proud of having done, and about what you have done that gave you a sense of accomplishment. Try to remember your personal successes. Being specific, list your positive accomplishments and what you like about yourself.

Study your past accomplishments and try to determine how you achieved them. Were you able to do things you didn't think you could do? What special abilities did you tap? Did you gain greater appreciation of your strengths? And finally, how can you use your strengths and abilities to accomplish what you want for yourself in the future.

DECISIONS AND SELF-ACCEPTANCE

Choosing future goals and values is a complex, always changing process. Dag Hammarskjold, former Secretary-General of the United Nations, reflected on the process of choosing:

At every moment you choose yourself. But do you choose

your self? Body and soul contain a thousand possibilities out of which you can build many *I's*. But in only one of them is there a congruence of the elector and the elected. Only one—which you will never find until you have excluded all those superficial and fleeting possibilities of being and doing with which you toy, out of curiosity or wonder or greed, and which hinder you from casting anchor in the experience of the mystery of life, and the consciousness of the talent entrusted to you which is your *I*.[5]

Finding your "I," accepting yourself, allows you to build a firm foundation for an intimate relationship. This chapter concludes with a listing, by psychiatrist Eugene McDanald and his associates, of some of the characteristics of a self-accepting person.

The self-accepting person is a participant in life rather than a spectator.

He is inclined to be objective, spontaneous, and emotionally and intellectually honest.

He tries to understand the interpersonal and environmental problems he faces, but he also accepts his limitations in gaining true insight concerning them.

He works out the best adjustment to life of which he is capable, often without fully understanding all that is involved.

However, he is willing to experience the pleasures and discomforts of self-revelation: i.e., he accepts the mixed pain and joy that accompany each change in his attitude and feeling toward himself and others.

His claims on life are, for the most part, reasonable. If he wants to be a member of the Country Club and yet cannot afford it, he finds other social and recreational outlets in keeping with his budget.

The self-accepting person without special talent or ability

is able to share emotionally in the gifts of others without undue regret about his inborn deficiencies.

He does not brood about missed opportunities, lost causes, errors, and failures. Rather, he looks on them for what they can contribute to his doing things differently or better in the future.

He does not get stuck in the rut of irrational feelings of love, hate, envy, jealousy, suspicion, lust, and greed, because he lets each feeling spell out its special message for him.

Although the self-accepting person may prefer not to be alone or isolated from family or friends, yet, in special times, when aloneness or isolation is a necessity, he can endure lack of contact with his fellows.

The self-accepting person may or may not be conventional in his thinking, feeling, or behavior. But when he is unconventional, it is not for the purpose of flaunting convention but rather for the sake of expressing or fulfilling a valid personal or public need.

He is not rigidly guided by rules and moralisms; hence he is willing to alter values in keeping with new insights.

He grants to others their right to values not identical with his own.

The self-accepting person puts himself into life in terms of his highest insights. Yet he accepts the fact that, in its essence, it remains the mystery of mysteries.[6]

Loving can cost a lot but not loving always
costs more, and those who fear to love
often find that want of love is an emptiness
that robs the joy from life.

MERLE SHAIN[1]

RISKING, TRUSTING, SHARING

chapter three

With a thoughtful, sad look on his face, David, a 36-year-old typesetter, begins to describe his experience:

> I had been married ten years to a woman who I really thought I loved, and I thought she loved me. Then all of a sudden—well, maybe not all of a sudden, but when it happened it seemed like all of a sudden—she rejected me and no longer cared for me. She wanted a divorce.
>
> And then there wasn't any way of turning the pain off. I kept living in the past even though I realized it was a bad thing to do.
>
> I had a desire for a warm body and I had a desire for sex, but at the same time I didn't really, because I was afraid of the possibility of falling in love with somebody, getting deeply involved again, and then getting hurt again. I shut myself off after my divorce. It was about six months before I even went out with a woman. I made a decision then that I would never really get involved closely with another woman.
>
> I protect myself by trying not to get too turned on and by shutting out part of my feelings. What I usually do is explain to the woman that I've been through a long marriage and that I've been hurt and that I don't want to

get into another relationship. But then what they usually say is if you're going to have a relationship, you should make it as good as you can while you've got it. But I have mixed feelings about that because once a relationship gets going the momentum will not allow me to stop and the first thing you know I've gotten so deep into it that I don't want to get out of it.

Four years ago I met a woman, and it was so nice that I was caught in it and we lived together for three years. The involvement scared me, but Ellen kept saying, "Hang loose—if we've got a good relationship, enjoy it while it's lasting. Don't worry about what it's going to lead to— enjoy it while it's here!" But I found that hard to accept, which is ridiculous because if you don't accept that then you can't have a relationship.

I did tell Ellen I loved her. But I felt that every time I said "I love you" or "I really care for you," it would cause her to get into the relationship deeper and deeper, and I didn't want her to get that attached to me, because if things didn't work out and if she'd gotten really attached to me then I would have to hurt her and hurt me at the same time in order to break it off.

Actually, what happened in the relationship with Ellen was that when it was dying out, I kept hanging on while she wanted to go.

To protect myself now, I'm not getting into a relationship. I don't need to be hurt again.

To love is to risk, and when you offer yourself you can be rejected. But if protecting against hurt becomes the overriding concern, higher levels of intimacy become unattainable.

Like many couples, David and Ellen had an unwritten pact to keep intimacy low, for both felt that if involvement were deep, breaking off their relationship could cause too much psychological pain. In support of this position they could cite the hurt that had resulted from their first marriages, the pain experienced by friends who had been hurt in love, the low percentage of enduring love relationships, and the high divorce rate. But by erecting protective barriers, they were limiting the intensity of both positive and negative feelings.

Other individuals, like Susan, whose story follows, react in the opposite direction with romantic fantasies that cannot possibly be fulfilled. Plunging into love, they view the relationship as they would like it to be rather than the way it actually is. Understandably, in a world that has much uncertainty and doubt, the illusion of certainty about another person may be alluring. But as with teenage infatuations, when a feeling of love is placed on a fantasy object, the illusion is destined to collapse.

Susan, a 28-year-old French teacher, reflected on an experience several years back:

> The first love of my life was the most romantic love of my life. Over a period of two weeks I realized I was in love with this person, even though I did not really know a lot about him or that much about myself. After several months I was living for this man, thought that things would work out and that he would sweep me off my feet, take me away, marry me, and that everything would be beautiful. Looking back, things weren't going that well but I was not willing to see that—as if I was as blind as a potato.
>
> Then I found out indirectly that the man with whom I was in love was sleeping with another woman. My sister, after some hemming and hawing, finally gave me the story and I was completely destroyed. It was the first time that I had ever contemplated suicide.
>
> So I decided to see a psychiatrist, and the first thing I said to the psychiatrist was I was contemplating suicide. A man had jilted me; I was very depressed; I didn't know what to do; and I just wanted to commit suicide. The first

thing he said was really funny—not at the time, of course—"Well, why don't you consider killing him rather than yourself?" It was the perfect answer and it made me start thinking a little bit more about myself and my own goals, of which I had none.

Selecting an appropriate partner is an important first step in approaching intimacy. Many personal factors, some conscious and some unconscious, enter into the decisions made by two people to begin or to intensify a relationship. The more realistic the reasons for selecting a partner, the greater the chances for the relationship to be successful.

Less hope for success exists when a person chooses a partner because of a strong desire to rescue or to be rescued. Wanting to help an intimate is a natural impulse, but the person who indulges in the rescue fantasy of making everything right for the partner may be striving for self-glorification. The intimate, in turn, may luxuriate in the fantasy that he or she can turn over all responsibility to the rescuer. Many people succumb to the fantasy that they can cure, convert, or miraculously transform their intimate. The rescuer feels mature and well-adjusted, and often relishes the position of superiority and control. People in the helping professions—especially counselors and psychotherapists— are often drawn like magnets to partners with emotional problems, believing that through their love and wisdom they will be able to make the other person happy.[2] Alcoholics and their partners are often involved in similar fantasy transactions. And popular lore still holds out the fantasies of the rescuing knight on a white horse or the all-understanding earth mother. Relationships based on such fantasies usually fail.

Francine, an attractive 25-year-old woman, took a calculated risk in her choice of a second husband. Her first marriage was never consummated because she experienced vaginismus, a sexual dysfunction in which the muscles of the outer vagina tightly constrict, making intercourse impossible. Psychologically, she refused to trust any man, risked as little as possible in her marriages, and equated participating in sexual intercourse with making herself vulnerable to exploitation. Her second husband was a man who made few sexual demands upon her, and his patient attitude gave her time to test his commitment and to learn to trust him. Eventually she was able to have sexual intercourse with him. By choosing so that the odds were in her favor, she was able to trust and to become more involved with her intimate.

DEVELOPING TRUST

When you are deeply involved with an intimate, you are vulnerable to psychic pain if that person uses or exploits you. How can you decide how much of yourself to risk? How does trust develop?

Trust develops gradually. Instant trust lacks firmness. You don't know how it will stand up under pressure since it has not been tested. The process of developing trust can be compared to peeling an onion. As the outer layers are removed, it becomes possible to go deeper and deeper. And in both people and onions, the outer layers provide protection.

One way of determining whether you can trust a partner is by gradually divulging areas of emotional sensitivity. These can include such things as experiences from your past, feelings of inadequacy, concerns about physical appearance. If the material you share is used against you, then both sharing and trust suffer. Only if your partner respects your minor sensitivities can you comfortably begin to reveal deeper emotional vulnerabilities. As trust, caring, and respect grow, you can reveal more personal and embarrassing parts of yourself, with less fear that the disclosures will be used against you.

Trust also can develop in a relationship when *both* partners divulge personal material. Reciprocity encourages sharing, provides protection, and supports the flow of open communication. Often, individuals who experience an intense crisis situation together reveal themselves deeply and as a result immediately feel very close. The *New York Times* reported an extreme example of this—an "instant" romance that took place during the power failure of 1965. In a stalled commuter train, a man and a woman who had met a few hours before asked the conductor to marry them.[3]

Another way of determining how much to trust is to observe the discrepancies between what your partner says and what your partner does. What do your past experiences with him indicate?* Has your partner demonstrated that he will stand by his word? Has his actual behavior shown that you can trust him? Or is the opposite true? Has he let you down? Has he done what he said he wouldn't do? Has he abused your trust? Or perhaps he tried to create the illusion that he would eventually satisfy your expectations, a pattern demonstrated by Cindy in her relationships.

> Every man who met Cindy at a party declared her absolutely charming, and went home somewhat disconsolately with his own date or wife. The men who knew her better were even more enchanted, though considerably more frustrated.
>
> Carl knew her as the perfect sex partner. She liked everything just the way he did, and seemed delighted to

---

*Here the masculine pronouns are used for convenience only; of course these questions can and should be asked of both female and male partners.

share all his little idiosyncrasies. Besides, she generously ignored the fact that he was a threadbare Ph.D. candidate, and could provide her with scarcely any other entertainment. But Carl was an attractive man and a good lover. He had no trouble finding sex. What really enchanted him was the way she shared his fascination with astronomy. She kept saying that she wanted to go to evening lectures with him, to help edit and type his thesis and to learn from him. Sadly, her efforts to survive as a painter, her long hours of work, and her part-time jobs had not yet permitted this. But soon—

At the same time, Larry, who owned the largest art gallery in town, appreciated Cindy's work as an assistant in preparing shows and handling customers. She was the only employee he permitted to work part time, and whose paintings he would sell. The poor girl had no time to share Larry's great passion, music. At least not just now. It was a rare thing to find an art talent who understood his feelings about music. They had many plans to attend concerts, to listen to the Ring Cycle on records of a winter weekend, but the plans remained just plans. . . .

Cindy was not consciously defrauding these men who were providing for so many of her needs. The con man, or woman, in love is rarely guilty of vicious intent, and tends to be the victim of his own dreams. [Either] of the men could have stopped Cindy's game by asserting specific demands.

"Exactly when, today, are we going to—?" was the only realistic question they had to ask. Probably they sensed this, but demurred for fear of breaking a comfortable illusion. After all, they were using Cindy to supply their dream needs.[4]

Another subtle form of exploitation, which again can usually be prevented by raising the appropriate questions, is the "as if" relationship. In the "as if" relationship at least one of the partners is incorrectly assuming that certain commitments exist. Harriet, a giving type of lover, experienced such a relationship for six months before realizing the situation. After she and Harvey broke up, she became aware of what had been going on.

"It seems like I was always the one who was giving a little bit more; and he took. The more that I gave, and the more that he took, the less respect he was giving me. Unfortunately I didn't figure that out until a long time after we split. I always figured he'd do something for me later."

Events that occurred that summer made Harriet realize that only the illusion of intimacy existed.

> He was giving up his apartment because he was going to travel for the summer, but he wanted to stay in town a couple more weeks. So I told him he could stay with me for a week or two. He moved in and it just didn't seem as if he was going to move out. I never asked for anything and I paid for all the groceries. He stayed for about five weeks and it was take, take, take on his part.
>
> I think the real clincher was one day when I was angry and I said, "Just where do you think this relationship is going?" He said he didn't want any permanent commitment kind of thing. And I thought here you are eating my food, living in my apartment, and not doing a damn thing for me. I said, "What are you wasting my time for?" and finally asked him to leave.
>
> Looking back, I think I didn't figure out what was happening at the time because of inexperience and because I wouldn't use another person like that. Because I wouldn't do it, I thought someone I was close to wouldn't do it either. In the future, I'm going to check things out little by little, step by step.

Many couples ignore potential problem areas and do not discuss important issues. Too often, the partners are reluctant to assess where they are in their relationship. By checking out your assumptions, and by being aware of what your partner says and does, you can gain a better idea of the status of your relationship. If you are willing to share your own feelings and to ask the right questions, and if your intimate is willing to answer honestly, you both will learn more about your relationship.

But many couples wonder whether the best strategy is to admit love or to play hard to get. Elaine and William Walster in *A New Look at Love* pondered and researched this question. They state,

> Socrates, Ovid, the *Kama Sutra,* Bertrand Russell, and "Dear Abby" all agree: love is stimulated by excitement and challenge. To find authors in such rare accord is refreshing. Unfortunately (but fortunately for the rest of us), it looks as if the sages were wrong. In the early 1970s, when we first began our investigations, we assumed that the sages were right. We accepted cultural lore.[5]

But the five experiments the Walsters and their associates conducted revealed that men liked the hard-to-get women and the easy-to-get women equally well.[6] In their book they ask:

> How, then, should we behave? Should we admit to others that we love them (thus offering them security)? Or should we play hard to get? The best answer seems to be: Act naturally. It's impossible to predict what others will like: some people are attracted to the candid, friendly type; others prefer those who are coolly aloof. There's nothing to be gained from *playing* at one role or another, so you might as well speak frankly and act freely. Express your admiration for those you like, your hopes for the relationship—and any doubts you have about either one.[7]

Research on the styles of loving shows some trends, but even these findings are subject to individual differences. Generally, game-players, stimulated by excitement and challenge, respond most enthusiastically to the hard-to-get person. Erotic, possessive, and practical types usually respond favorably to statements of love from their intimates. With the giving and friendship types, either way might be appropriate.

SHARING

Even if love and trust develop, the question remains whether to reveal or to keep personal secrets. Growth is stimulated by becoming aware of and then disclosing unacceptable parts of one's own self. Actually doing this, however, is more difficult than it sounds. In Sam's case a disturbing recurrent sexual fantasy forced him to deal with the "unacceptable" parts of his self.

At 35, Sam was a successful engineer involved in the construction of nuclear power plants. A big, well-built, good-looking man, he gave the appearance of competence and self-confidence. But Sam quickly told of having problems getting close to people, and said that he couldn't visualize a lasting relationship with a woman. Divorced twice, he wanted but felt incapable of having a successful marriage. He was currently dating a woman he regarded as his best friend ever, but he feared getting closer to her.

Sam entered psychotherapy mainly because a disturbing sexual fantasy had been coming into his thoughts with increasing frequency. It involved being dominated by an older, mature woman who was smarter, stronger, and bigger than he. She usually was wearing a bra, panties, a garter belt, and high heels. He said:

> She dominates me physically, eats me up, ties me to the bed. She forces me to be her servant, kiss her foot, or to orally stimulate her. She's in control and may even decide to masturbate me rather than to have intercourse. Occasionally she slaps me but usually there is no violence other than pinning me through wrestling or tying me down. She sometimes forces me to wear her panties. I find this fantasy very disturbing and am ashamed of it.

This fantasy and Sam's feelings that he needed more self-confidence were in sharp contrast to his image of super-competence and to his actual success at work. During his two marriages, he was referred to as Super Sam, and many of his friends view him as Super Sam, a man who can do virtually anything and who will come through in crises. Sam felt the need to project a very masculine appearance and felt he had to hide his feelings of inadequacy. He reflected, "Even as a child, I was anxiously awaiting becoming an adult so I could be successful. No one has ever told me what to do. Perhaps that's why in fantasy I am looking for someone to tell me what to do."

A few weeks later, Sam described the following dream:

> Somebody predicted that a great problem would be solved by a super animal which would devour two other animals, and I had the animal. Then I was in a room with famous people and cleverly revealed to them that I had the animal. They were looking to me for guidance. Then I felt as if I was in a trance and my voice was taken over and I then barely said "Help," and then it got a little bit louder—"*Help.*" I had on a dress. Even though I was me, I was a matriarch. All I could say was "Help."

This dream indicated that his feminine side was crying out for help. In his attempts to live up to the Superman image, Sam tried to suppress aspects of his weaknesses, his sensitivities, and his feminine side, but suppressed material has a way of coming out in dreams and fantasies.

Sam had a good relationship with his girlfriend Karen, and felt that she was the best friend he had ever had; he even revealed his disturbing fantasy to her. But, he said:

> I feel that I cannot tell her about my weakness and self-doubt. She has seen me as a very strong, competent, masculine person. She looks to me for advice, and although she is competent, she sees me as super-strong. I see her as both a friend and a lover. She is a friend, she is sexually interested in me, and she also comes to me for advice and makes me feel fatherly and powerful. And I do enjoy doing for people.

Sam was afraid to reveal his feelings of weakness to Karen, fearing that she wouldn't love him if she knew. Finally, after much encouragement in psychotherapy, he decided that he would take the risk. He poured out his feelings of self-doubt and inadequacy to Karen. Much to his surprise, she said "I love you even more now. You're more of a person to me now, and besides—I think I knew of those feelings all along." Sam's love for Karen increased as a result of his being able to really be himself. He said, "I feel a little of the Superman pressure to do everything well has been taken off me. It's been a big effort to appear self-confident, independent, and competent even when I have feelings of weakness." With the acceptance of his weaker side, Sam's fantasy dissipated and his relationship with Karen reached new levels of intimacy.

We all have a yearning to be understood. When we let down facades and when we divulge who we really are, then we reach a much deeper level of relating. To be loved fully after exposing one's true, authentic self can be both comforting and erotic. Intimacy flourishes as a result of sharing and feeling understood. Movie star Robert Redford experienced such sharing and understanding:

> Before I met Lola, I traveled. It was a great education in a lot of ways, but I felt a terrible low in Italy. I was completely alone and I felt like I'd aged and become an old man. No one I knew could relate to the feeling of isolation I had and I started drinking worse than ever. After Italy I went back in 1957 to California—that's where I come from. Lola was just out of high school and her attitude was so fresh and responsive. I had so much to say to her, that I started talking, sometimes all night long. She was genuinely interested in what I had to say, at a time when I really needed to talk.
>
> There were nights when we would walk around Hollywood Hills and start talking, like after dinner, walk down Hollywood Boulevard to Sunset, then up Sunset to the top of the hills, then over to the Hollywood Bowl and back to watch the dawn come up—and we'd still be talking. I had always said I'd never get married before I was 35, but my instincts told me that this was a person I'd like to go through life with.[8]

HOW MUCH DISCLOSURE IS BEST?

When intimates expose personal thoughts and feel understood by each other, love grows. But are some secrets best left untold? Are there times when discretion is best? Is disclosing certain thoughts detrimental to the relationship? Although most intimates would benefit from sharing more of their secrets with each other, the exact answers to the above questions are different for different relationships and for different styles of loving.

The lovestyle of the intimates influences the type and the extent of personal sharing. Many friendship lovers, like Arthur and Linda, who have a committed monogamous relationship, have no secrets. "Our lives are an open book to each other," says Linda. Giving lovers also accept honesty well, and can be forgiving if necessary. But possessive lovers, plagued by jealousy and preoccupied with thoughts about the beloved, are oversensitive to both past occurrences and potential threats. Practical lovers deal well with past indiscretions and want to solve everyday problems, but they carefully evaluate information that will affect their relationship in the future. For game-playing lovers, the indiscretions and secrets of a partner will in some instances be exciting, in other instances repelling; but they will in all cases be viewed as valuable information for devising future game-playing strategies—which under certain circumstances could be used against the partner. Erotic lovers want to know and to understand all that is related to the sex life and to the background of their intimate, but often avoid asking about unromantic personal facts (such as the details of a partner's illness). And within each style of loving, the amount of personal sharing is related to the amount of trust.

When trust exists, sharing personal vulnerabilities and feelings of inadequacy actually enhances togetherness. Many individuals, like Sam, who reluctantly disclose vulnerabilities, are surprised and relieved by the acceptance and understanding shown by their intimate. As a result all communication improves and it becomes easier to share feelings.

Honest sharing may be more difficult and more

complicated in the area of sex. Yet good lovemaking is closely linked with good communication. Sex therapist Helen Singer Kaplan says that trying to be an effective lover without communication is like trying to learn target shooting blindfolded.[9] Intimates have to learn what pleases them, and through honest sharing they can become more in tune sexually. By creating an atmosphere that encourages caring, acceptance, and spontaneity, and by specifically discussing at appropriate times what they find erotic, intimates add to the adventure of lovemaking.

A very different situation can occur when blunt truths are blurted out at the wrong time. Even among people who consider themselves liberated, problems can result from the spontaneous sharing of sexual fantasies at inappropriate moments. During passionate lovemaking, Nancy Friday fantasized being "fucked" by the man behind her at a football game as they both stood watching Johnny Unitas run for a touchdown. And just then her real lover spoke:

> "Tell me what you are thinking about," the man I was actually fucking said, his words as charged as the action in my mind. As I'd never stopped to think before doing anything to him in bed (we were that sure of our spontaneity and response), I didn't stop to edit my thoughts. I told him what I'd been thinking. He got out of bed, put on his pants and went home.[10]

Fantasies during intercourse and sexual fantasies about past lovers may be difficult to share with an intimate. Extramarital affairs may also be difficult to disclose, and many couples have an agreement that they don't want to know. Confessing sexual indiscretions when the partner does not ask and does not want to know may be using honesty as brutality.

Each couple must decide the extent to which they

will divulge secrets and be honest with each other. If there is a high level of trust, then a deep level of sharing will usually be best for the relationship. Intimates, in general, discover that they are able to disclose far more personal secrets than they thought possible. The key is trust. In trusting and being trusted, couples know and grow together.

> *[The] miraculous capacity which love*
> *bestows on the lovers consists in the power*
> *to discover in the object of love virtues*
> *which it actually possesses but which are*
> *invisible to the uninspired.*

OSWALD SCHWARTZ[1]

KNOWING
AND
ENHANCING
EACH OTHER

chapter four

During breakfast at a marriage and family counseling conference, an experienced marriage counselor told me:

> After I sit through a few sessions with each partner pointing his or her finger at the other and saying what he or she does that causes the trouble, and it looks as if its going to continue, I stop them and suggest an exercise. I never let them know about this exercise ahead of time. Then I say, "I want each of you to take five minutes and just talk about the things you like about your partner." This exercise usually throws them. I have yet to find a couple who are constantly bitching about each other who are able to talk for five minutes about the things they like about each other; and it embarrasses the hell out of them. And I just sit there and remain quiet for the five minutes, except I don't allow them to place any qualifying ifs, ands, or buts on their positive statements.
>
> Interestingly enough, couples start changing really fast after that. They realize there are positive things which they have been ignoring. So often they tell it to the partner for the first time in the session. Just last week a man said, "Things have been rough and we don't see the good things enough."

When partners appreciate and enhance each other, their relationship is stimulated. Like fertilizer fed to a plant, appreciation promotes growth. The first step, however, involves getting to know each other better.

The best way to learn more about your partner is to ask and to listen. Whether you have been married for twenty years or have known each other less than a week, the basic concept remains the same: You have to get beyond the superficial small-talk often used as a substitute for conversation.

Little communication takes place during brief meetings involving cliché greetings and forgettable small-talk. Barbara Walters comments:

> I know a girl who swears she went through an entire cocktail party replying gaily "I'm dying" whenever anyone asked "How are you?" All evening long people responded with "That's good; you certainly look great." She was amused at first but later awfully depressed at the whole business.[2]

We are more likely to speak honestly and openly about ourselves when the other person really listens. We all have a need to share ourselves, and we are most able to reveal our deeper feelings when we have a trusted intimate who accepts and understands.

Some people resist divulging personal information and give the following stock excuses:

> "It's best to keep them guessing a little."
>
> "It's not as exciting if you tell all."
>
> "You can't be both lovers and friends."
>
> "My mother says you should never put all your cards on the table."
>
> "What he/she doesn't know won't hurt him/her."

Encounter-group leader Jerry Gillies observes that many people fear that the joy of discovery will be gone and that boredom will set in once they bare their souls to an intimate. He believes that the lover who tries to maintain the mystery by withholding information is like a maiden who holds onto her virginity until she's fifty and then wonders why no one wants this precious gift.[3] When intimates increase the depth and the scope of their communications network, they expand the horizons of their relationship.

Frequently, at the beginning of a relationship, partners avoid important and sensitive questions. They assume roles as a way of protecting themselves. They present an image—which may include their possessions, manners, family background, educational accomplishments, social contacts, and occupation—as a way of attractively packaging and presenting themselves. Following a role or coming across as a member of an acceptable group reduces anxiety and provides protection—but it also slows down the development of intimacy. In the case of Barbara, a chance act of spontaneity broke down barriers. Barbara, a 26-year-old nurse, explains:

> We had been dating off and on for about a year in a friendly-only relationship. I think we both liked each other very much but there was an extreme formality which had prevented us from getting to know each other better. He always called at least a week in advance to ask me out. Well, this time he called on the spur of the moment and asked me if I'd like to go to lunch and a movie. The call woke me up, and I sleepily said, "No! I wouldn't like to go anywhere at all. Why don't you come over here?"
>
> I was surprised at saying this because I had never asked him to just come over. The apartment was a total wreck and I felt awkward about that, because it had always been

spotless when he had been over before. He came, and we had a terrific time. He was so different, and I was so different. We had always been dressed up and formal with each other. This time we were casual. We talked for about five or six hours. He told me about a lot of things that were really bothering him. I felt a lot closer to him than I have ever felt before.

By dropping facades and by allowing roles to change, Barbara and her friend finally became closer. Other individuals, however, resist changing unproductive ways of relating. The following case shows the perils of clinging to a self-defeating pattern.

Diane, a strikingly attractive 28-year-old school teacher, had a quick mind, an engaging personality, and a sharp wit. Few people would have suspected that she had difficulty in relationships with men. But Diane told the members of the singles encounter group about her consistently unproductive relationships.

When Diane first came to Atlanta as a school teacher, she decided that she wanted to marry a wealthy man, and over the years she became more committed to this goal. In view of her beauty, intelligence, and personality, her objective was realistic. A frequent guest at one of the most exclusive private clubs in town, Diane socialized with rich people. For a five-year period she had intimate relationships with "appropiate" men, but the relationships never lasted. Last year she thought she had "the right man," even though he had never acknowledged the depth of their relationship, which she assumed he felt. Then, suddenly, he announced his plans to marry another woman. Diane felt devastated.

After several months of depression, Diane met Wesley, a 39-year-old lawyer from a wealthy and prominent family. Never married, Wesley told Diane not to view him as a potential marital partner. Diane stopped dating others;

Wesley did not make a similar commitment. He dated her only about two nights a week and often gave her little notice ahead of time. Diane didn't ask what he did the nights they weren't together—"that would be prying." But her curiosity made her play detective; she looked through Wesley's desk drawer while he was away. She discovered a letter from another woman. Angry at him for being involved with someone else, but feeling guilty with herself for going through his private items, Diane decided not to mention her find.

More significantly, Diane, reluctant to ask Wesley personal questions, emphasized to the group that she did not want to infringe on his privacy. The result: Wesley had divulged virtually nothing personal to her during eight months of dating. She suspected that his mother had an important influence on him, but felt it would be inappropriate to ask questions about his family: "that would be pushing him."

Group feedback centered on Diane's limited impact on Wesley and suggested that mutual sharing of personal information would produce greater intimacy. Diane rejected these suggestions, said she had Wesley figured out, and reasserted her beliefs that he could be neither pressured nor encouraged to share personal information.

Two months later, the relationship ended. Diane was angry. Wesley was bewildered by her deep resentment because he had never felt they had been that close.

Perhaps the woman Wesley will eventually marry will be able to elicit self-revelation from him and create an atmosphere in which secrets, hopes, fears, and other personal feelings can be shared.

In dating situations, some couples avoid sharing personal information in order to limit involvement. Other couples exclude large areas of conversation, while deluding themselves into thinking they have good communication.

Fred, for example, was a talkative and successful insurance executive, married ten years. He rarely discussed his business dealings with his wife. The few times he had spoken about his business, she listened attentively, found the details interesting, and encouraged further discussion. What prevented him from telling her more? He claimed that because of the competition in his field, business dealings were best kept confidential, and he described an incident in which he had helped a new colleague only to have the information he shared used against him a week later. But had his wife ever violated his confidence? "No, she wouldn't do that; I can trust her," he quickly replied. Fred then realized that, although he could not discuss competitive information with colleagues, he could talk about sensitive business dealings with his wife.

Another example comes from a woman, married nine years, who only recently discovered the benefits of better communication. She says:

> As a young wife staying home with my small children, I very often felt lonely, misunderstood, and, worst of all, taken for granted. My self-prescribed comfort was "That's all there is to a marriage—who's happy, anyway?" Since I didn't want to rock the boat or be ungrateful, I never worked up the courage to bring my loneliness to the attention of my "partner for life." I was raised in the belief that the less you talk about something, the less it is there. Since I did everything to conceal my misery, my husband thought for many years that I was as happy as he was, because at intervals we did have some good times together.
>
> It was he who finally suspected there should be more. So he started asking what my innermost feelings were. And that was the start of our opening up to each other, and trusting each other. It was a painful process getting everything out into the open, even though neither of us had cheated on the other. But we had finally found the

key—total trust and commitment in each other. Now we are very happy.

As the last two examples illustrate, talking about areas of mutual interest and concern helps a relationship. There is a type of talking, however, that hurts a relationship—nagging. The nagger can talk incessantly, can generate hostility, and can drive the partner away. Nagging is the opposite of good communication, and its destructive effect is chronicled in the following historical account by Dale Carnegie.

> ... Napoleon III of France, nephew of Napoleon Bonaparte, fell in love with Marie Eugénie Ignace Augustine de Montijo, Countess of Teba, the most beautiful woman in the world— and married her. His advisors pointed out that she was only the daughter of an insignificant Spanish count. But Napoleon retorted: "What of it?" Her grace, her youth, her charm, her beauty filled him with divine felicity. In a speech hurled from the throne, he defied an entire nation: "I have preferred a woman I love and respect," he proclaimed, "to a woman unknown to me."
>
> Napoleon and his bride had health, wealth, power, fame, beauty, love, adoration—all the requirements for a perfect romance. Never did the sacred fire of marriage glow with a brighter incandescence.
>
> But, alas, the holy flame soon flickered and the incandescence cooled—and turned to embers. Napoleon could make Eugénie an empress; but nothing in all *la belle France,* neither the power of his love nor the might of his throne, could keep her from nagging.
>
> Bedeviled by jealousy, devoured by suspicion, she flouted his orders, she denied him even a show of privacy. She broke into his office while he was engaged in affairs of state. She interrupted his most important discussions. She

refused to leave him alone, always fearing that he might be consorting with another woman. . . .

. . . But neither royalty nor beauty can keep love alive amidst the poisonous fumes of nagging. Eugénie could have raised her voice like Job of old and have wailed: "The thing which I greatly feared is come upon me." Come upon her? She brought it upon herself, poor woman, by her jealousy and her nagging.

Of all the sure-fire, infernal devices ever invented by all the devils in hell for destroying love, nagging is the deadliest. It never fails. Like the bite of the king cobra, it always destroys, always kills.

The great tragedy of Abraham Lincoln's life also was his marriage. Not his assassination, mind you, but his marriage. When Booth fired, Lincoln never realized he had been shot; but he reaped almost daily, for twenty-three years, what Herndon, his law partner, described as "the bitter harvest of conjugal infelicity." "Conjugal infelicity?" That is putting it mildly. For almost a quarter of a century, Mrs. Lincoln nagged and harassed the life out of him.

She was always complaining, always criticizing her husband; nothing about him was ever right. He was stoop-shouldered, he walked awkwardly and lifted his feet straight up and down like an Indian. She complained that there was no spring to his step, no grace to his movement; and she mimicked his gait and nagged at him to walk with his toes pointed down, as she had been taught at Madame Mentelle's boarding school in Lexington.

She didn't like the way his huge ears stood out at right angles from his head. She even told him that his nose wasn't straight, that his lower lip stuck out, that he looked consumptive, that his feet and hands were too large, his head too small.

Did all this nagging and scolding and raging change Lincoln? In one way, yes. It certainly changed his attitude toward her. It made him regret his unfortunate marriage, and it made him avoid her presence as much as possible.[4]

Constantly focusing on a partner's negative characteristics can drive that person away. Frequently, couples emphasize faults, while they take virtues for granted. Not surprisingly, a recent study found that husbands and wives who had better marriages expressed more verbal affection, disclosed more personal facts, and provided more psychological encouragement and moral support for each other.[5]

ENHANCING ONE ANOTHER

Are you and your intimate aware of and able to express what is positive in your relationship? You might consider the following questions:

- What do you appreciate about each other?
- What problems from the past have been handled well?
- What happy and good experiences have you had together?
- What do you like about your relationship?
- What pleasant experiences do you enjoy together?
- What do you each do in everyday life to show your caring?
- What things does your intimate do which make you feel loved or appreciated?
- What future hopes do you as a couple share?

Intimates can enhance each other's self-awareness and self-esteem. When partners relate with understanding, appreciation, and interest, they feel more psychologically alive and their uniqueness is confirmed. They may even discover new parts of themselves, as the following account by a 35-year-old businessman shows:

> Cathy makes me feel unique because she looks inside me and sees things in me that no one else has ever seen. She's able to see the things that are creative, that are not fitting a mold. She's like a catalyst for me; she draws me out. I never thought I was creative or that I could write well. She kept saying, "You're creative, you can do things you've never done before." She actually made me feel that way. Damn, I actually wrote some poems to her. And then it began to be fun to write and to do things that I had never done or felt that I could do.

Intimates are in a position to appreciate each other's uniqueness. They may have special abilities, qualities, or idiosyncracies that are known only to their partners. For example, Dave's wife Marion pictures herself as a mature, aggressive, businesslike career woman, and tries to maintain this appearance. Yet Dave loves her occasional "little-girl" behavior which she expresses privately only with him. Dave recalls:

> One day Marion was out of town on an important business trip. A few nights before she left we had been to the movies and she had bought a lot of junk food to munch during the movie. I have always teased her about doing this because it is so out of character for her and so like the "little-girl" part of her that only I know. While she was away, I kept noticing her box of candy "Dots" she had left

on the coffee table. Now what adult really eats "Dots"! Every time I passed the table I would have warm feelings toward her. Finally I sat down and picked up the box of Dots, held it and looked at it for a while, thinking warm and loving feelings toward my nutty but very bright wife. I felt very close to her even though she was far away. Finally, for the hell of it, I popped a Dot into my mouth, and went on about my work smiling and feeling that Marion was right there in the house with me.

IMPROVING COMMUNICATION

To say that couples need more communication is like saying that poor people need more money. Seeing the problem is easy; solving it more difficult. Our society offers guidelines for everyday, superficial social conversation, but couples living together require deeper, more sensitive levels of relating in which they can exchange feelings, expectations, hopes, fears, and personal needs.

The deepest type of intimate communication requires sharing your feelings openly and honestly, without blaming or attacking your partner and without defending yourself. Although doing this is neither easy nor natural, when it is actually accomplished it promotes intimacy and validates togetherness. As a first step, you and your intimate might try the following exercise. Write down a few areas of your relationship in which communication is good. Then list areas of your relationship in which communication is poor. Finally, allow an hour for discussing the lists.[6] Try to listen, to understand, to share feelings. Emphasize understanding, rather than blaming or defending.

Some couples, at times, communicate effectively through written notes. By writing your partner a letter, you can thoughtfully formulate what you want to say. Your intimate will also have time to think about and respond to your written thoughts. Writing down your ideas and feelings allows you to express something on your mind, to ponder the issue, and to explore possible solutions.

No matter what the method of communication, the goal is increased understanding of each other. Look at your relationship and think about the following two questions:

- What makes you feel understood?
- What can your intimate do to help you identify and share your inner thoughts and feelings?

These are difficult questions which you both might consider discussing, because the answers provide a valuable key to communication.

With increased communication, intimates get more satisfaction from their relationship and discover more possibilities for growth. Deeper relating occurs as each partner becomes more aware of the other. In a study on communication and marital satisfaction, Leslie Navran found that happily married people differ from those who are unhappily married in the following ways (in descending order of importance):

1. Much more frequently talk over pleasant things that happen during the day.
2. Feel more frequently understood by their spouses; that is, that their messages are getting across.
3. Discuss things which are shared interests.

4. Are less likely to break communication off or inhibit it by pouting.

5. More often will talk with each other about personal problems.

6. Make more frequent use of words which have a private meaning for them.

7. Generally talk most things over together.

8. Are more sensitive to each other's feelings and make adjustments to take these into account when they speak.

9. Are more free to discuss intimate issues without restraint or embarrassment.

10. Are more able to tell what kind of day their spouses have had without asking.[7]

The list indicates the importance of communication; notice that it includes *no* items which involve meaningless chatter or talking for the sake of talking. Study and think about these ten crucial items.

I was angry with my friend:
I told my wrath, my wrath did end.
I was angry with my foe:
I told it not, my wrath did grow.

WILLIAM BLAKE

FACING
CONFLICT
EFFECTIVELY

chapter five

77

"The fundamental cause of marital failure in our time is the inability to resolve the anger which is inevitably generated in an intimate relationship," observes David Mace, a marriage counselor for almost forty years. Drawing on his experiences in seventy-four countries, Dr. Mace concludes that relationships fail because of "the incapacity of the couple to cope with their own and each other's anger."[1]

With increased intimacy comes greater potential for anger and more vulnerability to hurt. Accepting this basic fact helps in understanding conflict. Moreover, recent research continues to confirm what William Blake knew long ago—unexpressed anger grows. This chapter, drawing on developments in research and psychotherapy, will present a method for facing conflict effectively.

"PEACE" AT WHAT PRICE?

Many "peaceful" relationships appear good to friends of the couple, but become intolerable to the actual participants. A newspaper story, occasionally mentioned by marriage counselors, describes a woman bewildered by her husband's behavior. During fifteen years of marriage he had never raised his voice, uttered a harsh word, or complained about her behavior. She said she had no idea that he was dissatisfied with any aspect of their relationship. One day she came home and found a note: "I'm leaving forever. I can't stand it anymore."

This story illustrates the cultural taboo against anger. Many couples refuse to face conflict because of the tension, guilt, and anxiety they would feel if they acknowledged the discord. Afraid and ashamed of their anger, they let resentments, tensions, and grievances accumulate, rather than trying to talk about what is wrong. Complete harmony becomes the ideal. But by trying to maintain peace at any price, they sacrifice important individual wants and needs, bringing stagnation and boredom to their relationship. A decline in sexual feelings usually follows because self-expression and self-assertion are vital for passion. In fact, when perfect harmony is the goal, all forms of intimate communication occur less frequently between the partners.

A pattern of repressing anger can develop from the fear of losing love and from past conditioning in childhood. Many children are brought up to believe it is wrong to feel angry. More common are people who fear that expressing any anger will drive a partner away and who allow this fear to increase as the intimate becomes more important to them. Afraid to admit anger or irritation, they overreact by feeling that even mildly expressed anger will be as disastrous as a huge fight. Consequently, commenting on an irritating personal habit of the partner seems too dangerous. Inevitably resentments accumulate.

Buried resentments block a couple from real intimacy, because suppression of negative feelings also reduces positive feelings. "A curious thing which never fails to surprise persons in therapy," Rollo May observes, "is that after admitting their anger, animosity, and even hatred for a spouse and berating him or her during the hour, they end up with feelings of love toward this partner. A patient may have come in smoldering with negative feelings but resolved, partly unconsciously, to keep these, as a good gentleman does, to himself; but he finds that he represses the love for the partner at the same time as he suppresses his aggression."[2] This pattern has been apparent in my counseling with couples. As negative feelings elicited by past hurts are expressed, much to the surprise of the couple, positive feelings also emerge.

Bill and Anne were such a couple. After ten years of marriage, they felt that their life together had become listless and boring. Anne wanted a separation, but since she feared the effect it would have on their two daughters, she agreed to marriage counseling instead.

During the first few sessions, Anne rarely expressed emotion or told how she felt. In an attempt to get at suppressed grievances that could be blocking feelings, I asked her to bring in a list of instances when she had been badly hurt by Bill over the years.

Much emotion surfaced as Anne discussed her six major resentments. The most important incident on her list occurred just before her marriage to Bill. They had dated steadily throughout high school, and at the beginning of their senior year Anne was shocked to discover she was pregnant. She had greatly resented the way Bill dealt with the situation. She said that he immediately discussed with his mother the question of whether or not to get married.

Moved by Anne's strong feelings, Bill told, for the first time, what he had actually done during those crucial hours. He had made the decision to marry Anne within a half hour. Only then did he discuss their situation with his mother in an effort to determine possible living arrangements. After discussing this major resentment, as well as other past hurts they both had, Bill and Anne regained some good feelings about their relationship.

Sidney's twenty-eight-year marriage had deteriorated. One of his problems was impotence. During the past year he had been able to have sexual relations with his wife only once. He told of a big argument preceding the sexual experience. As their fight was ending, Sidney and his wife felt passion for each other, and he unexpectedly developed a strong erection. Sidney's experience is not unusual. Good lovemaking often occurs after an argument. Expressing feelings of dissatisfaction and being understood makes a person feel alive and real, often heightening intimate communication and passion. When intimates expose themselves in a productive argument, they can sense their impact on each other.

Unacknowledged anger can come out indirectly and be confusing. Anger may be expressed passively by forgetting, sabotaging plans, and "unintentionally" causing problems. For example, Edward believed that expressing any negative feelings was not polite. He always told Carol that she was a "terrific person," even though he felt much resentment toward her. He displayed this resentment by expressing his anger indirectly. At the last minute he canceled a weekend they had planned together away from the children, an event Carol had been looking forward to for weeks. He frequently called from work in the evening to say he couldn't be home for dinner or attend a social function. Sexual relations or even physical touching were infrequent. Several days after Carol started a diet, she received candy as a surprise present from Edward.

By operating indirectly, the person using hidden aggression cloaks his activities with a seemingly caring motive and avoids an openly aggressive encounter. Dealing with this indirect expression of anger is difficult because of the guise of good intentions.

When Edward was confronted with his behavior, he was apologetic about the "coincidences" and repeated his intention to treat "a terrific person" like Carol with more consideration. But it turned out he was still simmering with anger from an incident that had occurred at their home over two years ago. During dinner with a potential business partner, Edward described what he thought to be an exciting business venture. In front of the guest, Carol criticized and made fun of the idea. Edward was furious with Carol that night and she knew it, but they have never discussed the incident. He thinks it would be "impolite" to bring up his resentments.

Never expressing anger directly can also result in psychosomatic symptoms. Fred, a meek man dominated by an aggressive wife and daughter, displayed his anger passively by sabotaging plans. But a rise in his blood pressure was a visible sign of what he was unable to verbalize. Researchers have consistently found that hostile feelings, when turned inward, can produce physical problems. Mismanaged anger can also generate guilt and depression.

DEALING WITH ANGER

Although repressing resentments and avoiding conflict are dangerous, the uncontrolled venting of anger can be even more destructive. Sharp, cutting criticism and physical abuse can destroy intimacy. Moreover, evidence indicates that as people allow themselves to vent anger, they become more prone to physical violence.[3] When one partner has a violent temper the other has to be on guard. In an intimate relationship, where the two people make themselves vulnerable, the unleashing of anger against each other is usually destructive. There are individuals, however, who do have masochistic leanings and seem to invite physical punishment. One patient complained of the beatings she received from her husband during his bouts of drinking. Significantly, this same pattern had existed in her two previous marriages.

Problems may arise from repressing, displacing, or venting anger. How can anger and conflict best be handled in an intimate relationship? Some insights emerge from research on conflict and a recent magazine survey.

A questionnaire on marriage was printed in *Redbook* magazine. About 75,000 women responded, and the following conclusions* were drawn on the topic of conflict:

> The women who are most satisfied with their marriages describe a relationship that is not the starry-eyed, adolescent, heaven-made version of marriage. In fact, couples who have the best relationships do admit to hacking over problems and worries and disagreeing with each other— but they disagree more or less agreeably.
>
> The majority of women argue with their husbands now and then about six general topics: irritating personal habits, money, their husbands' not showing them enough love, in-law conflicts, how to discipline the children, and sex. Six wives out of 10 argue at least occasionally about who does what around the house.
>
> What comes out of the whole range of questions about disagreements, however, is the strong sense that *how* husbands and wives express their disagreement is much more important than *what* they disagree about. We asked readers what they are most likely to do when they are displeased with their husbands and what their husbands

* Reprinted from Redbook Magazine, June 1976. Copyright © by The Redbook.

are most likely to do—say nothing, brood about it, hint that they're unhappy, express their feelings or start an argument. We also asked how often they and their husbands behave in these different ways when they do argue—leave the room, sulk, sit in silence, swear, shout, hit out, cry or break things.

The most happily married wives are those who say that *both* they and their husbands tell each other when they are displeased and thus try to work out their displeasure together by communicating in a calm and rational way. They also say that they and their husbands rarely or never fight in any of the different ways we listed; that is, they seldom resort either to the active-aggressive fighting (swearing, shouting, hitting out, crying or breaking things) or to passive-aggressive fighting (leaving the room, sulking or staying silent).

The wives who are most unhappily married are in relationships where one or both partners can't talk calmly about what's bothering them or when one or both do a lot of fighting in the traditional ways. If one partner tends to avoid a fight and the other is a fighter, they're just as likely to be unhappy as if both were fighters.[4]

An important conclusion arising from this study is that the *way* a couple expresses disagreement is more important than what they disagree about. Neither withdrawal from conflict nor vicious, aggressive fighting will work.

Anger expressed constructively can establish, restore, or maintain a close relationship. In the *Intimate Enemy* and in his other works,[5] psychologist George Bach describes a valuable system for "fair fighting." No chapter on conflict would be complete without including his concepts. But perhaps words such as "fighting" and "enemy" are misleading or too strong. Once a couple has mastered a good system for dealing with conflict, they will usually be preventing problems, rather than having true "fights."

Recent developments in psychotherapy and research indicate that certain techniques, when mastered, promote success in handling confrontations. In the following section, these techniques are presented as fourteen principles.

PRINCIPLES FOR FACING CONFLICT EFFECTIVELY

As with most skills, the ability to deal effectively with conflict develops through involvement, understanding, and practice. Applying these principles to your relationship might, to stretch an analogy a bit, be compared with learning to play tennis. A book on tennis will be helpful only if you practice the techniques outlined. Even then many principles will be difficult to master. Knowing all the steps required for an effective tennis stroke is much easier than performing them at the crucial moment. Often you will be aware of your mistakes, but you will require time for correcting them. At some stages learning a correct technique, perhaps a way of holding the racket, will at first be uncomfortable, but will become a good habit as it brings about more successful results. The initial self-consciousness inherent in following rules will gradually disappear as you gain proficiency through practice.

The principles described below are easy to read, but their application requires the involvement and the cooperation of both partners. A basic assumption is that you both are willing to work on improving your intimate relationship.

The following are the principles for effectively facing conflict:

Basic Ground Rules

1. Complain with a spirit of good will.
2. Avoid attacking each other.
3. Focus on the here and now.
4. Admit your feelings.

Specific Techniques

5. Select an appropriate time.
6. Be specific.
7. Deal with one issue at a time.
8. Ask for a reasonable change.
9. Listen carefully.
10. Try to accept and understand.

Finding a Solution

11. Think, explore, meditate.
12. Be willing to accept incomplete resolution.
13. Consider compromise.
14. Avoid trying to win.

1. COMPLAIN WITH A SPIRIT OF GOOD WILL

Acknowledge the importance of your relationship. Can you operate on the assumption that neither of you would intentionally hurt the other?

If you trust each other, you will not have to be afraid of your partner exploiting your weaknesses. In fact, dealing with conflict fairly usually increases mutual trust. A successful confrontation affirms how important a part you are in your intimate's life, and provides an opportunity to gain better understanding of yourself and your partner.

2. AVOID ATTACKING EACH OTHER

People have a collection of insults and sarcastic remarks that can be used instantly in disagreements. But sarcasm, insults, name-calling, criticism of relatives, and personality attacks elicit feelings of anger and revenge, as well as obscuring the issue under discussion. Once initiated, vicious attacks on a partner, although often regretted immediately afterwards, cannot be taken back. And the snowball effect of devastating criticism makes a fight increasingly vicious.

Especially harmful are insulting remarks and negative labels that undermine a person's self-esteem. Nobody appreciates being called "stupid," not to mention more derogatory labels. An individual who is repeatedly called "stupid" may eventually start feeling and behaving as if he or she were stupid.

3. FOCUS ON THE HERE AND NOW

What you are doing now is important. Rehashing old failures and disappointments is unproductive. By avoiding past history, the argument can focus on one issue in the here and now.

Going into the past is often a diversionary fight tactic. Yesterday's failures, dredged up and used as today's ammunition, may produce guilt and anger. But progress, not guilt, is what you want. So be willing to forgive your partner, or at least to believe that what happened last time does not necessarily have to happen again.

If you avoid imposing the past on the present or future, constructive change in your relationship becomes more likely, and the possibilities for overcoming irritations and stalemates increase. As the here-and-now relationship improves, the mistakes and disagreements from the past will probably become more understandable.

4. ADMIT YOUR FEELINGS

You are responsible for telling your partner if something is bothering you. Too many exchanges between intimates sound like the following:

> "What's wrong?"
>
> "Nothing!"
>
> "But you're stomping around and acting mad. What's wrong?"
>
> "If you don't know, there's no use telling you."

Even the most empathic of partners is not a mind-reader. Blaming your intimate for not "knowing" encourages unproductive dialogue.

In fact, at times you may be unable to determine the source of your disturbance. For example, negative feelings from fatigue or work problems may be displaced onto your intimate. Sorting out the components of an angry mood might be difficult, but talking about the anger is more constructive than venting it or letting it feed on itself. Try to become more aware of your feelings. What areas of your life generate concern? What effect do your partner's actions have on you?

Learning to talk clearly about feelings is difficult. One way of promoting honesty and clarity is to use personal "I" statements. Begin your sentences with the pronoun "I" ("I think . . . ," "I feel . . . ," "I need . . . ," "I like . . . ," "I would like to know what you . . . ,"). Such "I" statements tell about you and are self-representing rather than selfish.

However, opinionated "I" statements, such as "I think you . . . ," are not useful. The object is to discover and define your own feelings. The only mind you have full permission to read is your own.

5. SELECT AN APPROPRIATE TIME

Cooperative effort is more likely when a mutually convenient time is chosen for discussing a grievance. A future appointment gives you both an opportunity to reflect on your feelings and to organize your thoughts. Freedom from distractions and from other immediate obligations provides an environment in which more constructive exchanges can take place.

They were in bed at 1 A.M. and he had to catch an early plane that morning. She stiffened as he touched her. He (not knowing): "Is something wrong?" She: "Yes! There are some things you do that I want to talk to you about." He (nervously): "What?" At this point she unloaded a pile of grievances on him. Not surprisingly, in a situation such as this, a vicious, unproductive fight often occurs.

When your partner is fatigued, sick, or under special pressure, try to postpone dealing with the conflict. Unfortunately, irritation and conflict often emerge in just such stressful situations, and a "hit-and-run" attack might be tempting. One option is to admit that something is bothering you and to make a mutual promise to discuss the problem at a later and better time. This will allow both of you to reflect on your feelings, to decide what needs to be said, and to discuss the problem under better conditions. Sometimes the mutual admission of anger or irritation and the promise to discuss it will improve the situation immediately and provide hope for finding a solution.

People who are afraid of conflict, or who would rather snipe than solve the problem, regularly air annoyances when there is not enough time to explore the matter, or when the presence of other people or other distractions makes productive confrontation impossible. Such "hit-and-run" attacks make the situation worse. If possible, wait until you are alone and can spend some time talking.

6. BE SPECIFIC

Think about what made you angry. Focus on specific actions, feelings, and attitudes, and be as explicit as possible in describing the anger-producing situation for your partner. Good verbal or physical communication is understandable and thrives on the specific; generalities obscure the real problem between you and your partner.

Being specific is a prerequisite for clear communication. In his humorous article "The Vague Specific," Richard Gehman comments on his wife's tendency to refer vaguely to particular persons or events.

> "The men came today," she says.
>
> I can never tell which men she means, but I can never get up enough courage to ask. For a while, I had a system figured out to beat her at this game, but it backfired. The conversation went like this:
>
> *My wife:* The men came today.
>
> *Me* (craftily): What did you tell them?
>
> *My wife:* I told them to go ahead.

The only satisfaction I got from this was the knowledge that, whatever the men had gone ahead and done, it was going to cost me money.[6]

In ordinary day-to-day situations vague communication might be only mildly irritating, but in a disagreement with your partner, knowing what you are talking about is essential.

7. DEAL WITH ONE ISSUE AT A TIME

Try to determine your primary grievance. What is really bothering you? Is a trivial issue serving as a decoy? A seemingly absurd complaint may be camouflaging an important issue. You can deal more effectively with conflict by focusing on one grievance and avoiding other topics.

Gunny-sacking refers to storing up many unexpressed resentments. When the sack is finally opened, most of the complaints come out, but there are too many to deal with. Overloaded with grievances, the partners might become confused and angry, and both may feel that the situation is hopeless.

Gloria was a gunny-sacker. Periodically she would unload a barrage of minor complaints on her husband Winston. Overwhelmed by her criticism, Winston would become quiet and withdrawn, a reaction that elicited more browbeating and nagging from Gloria. Their anger would increase, and afterwards they would not speak to each other for days.

In counseling, Gloria again dumped a gunny-sack of complaints on Winston. After she finished, I encouraged her to go back and examine one issue at a time, and to try to determine what was really bothering her.

Finally, Gloria's real concern surfaced. With emotion

she said, "He's got to let me know he loves me. I have to feel he wants me and needs me. I want to be assured that I'm loved and needed." This one issue was Gloria's main concern. Most of the other grievances in her gunny-sack were indirect ways of trying to establish her importance in Winston's life. Winston had difficulty telling Gloria he loved and needed her, even though he did have these feelings. He thought she knew. Eventually he was able to tell Gloria how much she meant to him. When Gloria was reassured of Winston's deep commitment to their relationship, the issues that she had been complaining about became less significant.

8. ASK FOR A REASONABLE CHANGE

What do you really want from your partner? Is your request authentic and realistic? Simply complaining will not produce an effective solution. In fact, most criticism is unnecessary and damaging. For example, when Mary spilled nail polish on the floor, her husband yelled at her. Mary did not need criticism at this point; she felt bad enough already.

If a problem requires change, discuss possible solutions. Give your partner a chance to correct the situation. What can your intimate do?

A college student living with her boyfriend recalled the following:

> Before I started work and classes, I would cook and perform most of the household chores. After school began I was tired most of the time and dreaded coming home to dirty pots and pans each night. I was often too tired to enjoy the sex which had always been good between us.

We started to have little fights which began growing in intensity. My mood was often bad because I felt I was being used as a Suzie Homemaker object and because I was tired. Finally, during one of our fights, I said I was tired of playing the homemaker role and could use help around the house. We spoke about the situation, and Jim now prepares some meals and helps with some of the household chores. As a result of this, our situation has improved.

9. LISTEN CAREFULLY

Ask questions, give feedback, and check out your assumptions. Be able to restate what your partner has said. Avoid assuming you know what your partner is thinking or how he/she will react. Think about the feedback you have received. Did you become aware of new information? What else would you like to know? Hearing and remembering important messages may be difficult during the emotional arousal of many arguments. A tape recorder can help. By providing objective feedback, the tape recording can reveal the way you and your partner actually came across. Were major points heard, explored, and understood? Did interruptions interfere? Were issues discussed specifically and clearly? What behaviors might be preventing a better flow of communication?

Alvin, separated from his wife Linda, was continuing his affair with Rhonda. But he was unable to decide which woman he really wanted. Just before his separation, he had been certain of his love for Rhonda. She was the most aware and interesting woman he had ever met, and conversations with her were stimulating.

But lately the situation had changed. Rhonda had been losing interest in him, and they no longer had much to talk about. To confuse matters further, Alvin had started feeling closer to Linda and wanted counseling with her.

During their counseling sessions, Alvin asked Linda to assert herself more, to ask for what she wanted, and to discuss events between them. Linda agreed, but as she asserted herself, Alvin's temper flared. He would interrupt her before she was through talking and would criticize her feelings and actions before he fully heard them.

During individual therapy Alvin realized that his own behavior had suppressed conversation and the expression of feelings in his relationships with both Linda and Rhonda.

10. TRY TO ACCEPT AND UNDERSTAND

Be open to your partner's feelings. Accept them, even if they are very different from what you would feel in a similar situation.

The value of accepting an intimate's feelings is illustrated by the following statement from a 32-year-old woman:

> I've been married ten years and have two children. We base our marriage on openness and creative fighting, and we've found over the years the number of problems has reduced greatly. One guideline we use when working out difficulties is that your emotional feeling about something is every bit as valid as somebody else's action. For example, taking the classic trivia problem, I was the type of person who did not put the cap back on the toothpaste. It used to drive my husband up the wall. There was no question of whether or not it should drive him up the wall.

It was simply his legitimate feeling that it did. And so this is one way I gave in and changed over time because it made for a helpful situation.

Explore what your intimate is thinking and feeling, without putting him on the defensive by telling him how he should think or feel. And as much as possible, avoid using the word "Why." For most people, the simple word "Why" has been associated with overtones of blame and condemnation, and consequently elicits defensiveness.

Stick with the facts, rather than trying to attribute psychological motives and trying to read your partner's mind. Incorrect interpretations are anger-provoking. The "I know more about you than you do" attitude can be irritating. In this age of pop psychology, many people give unwanted interpretations which show a lack of understanding and block deeper communication.

Focus on understanding your partner's grievances and feelings. You can accept and explore your partner's point of view without changing your own. And if your intimate feels truly understood by you, she/he will be more receptive to your suggestions.

11. THINK, EXPLORE, MEDITATE

Have you learned something you didn't know before? Has all the information related to the problem been explored? Are you both fully aware of your attitudes? Make sure you are understanding each other.

Examine your feelings and think about what your intimate has said. As you verbalize your thoughts, new ideas may appear. What are the options? Would you be willing to consider a change?

You may need time to think about new information

your intimate has presented. Maybe a better solution to the problem will occur to one of you later. Would thinking about the issue and finishing the discussion in a day or two be helpful?

Henry, a 27-year-old engineer, enjoyed his high-paying job except for the required traveling. Joan's main complaint was that her husband was out of town more days than he was home. Henry was hoping that a coming promotion would cut down on the travel, but his assumption was unchecked. Much to his dismay, he found out that the new position would also require extensive travel. On the basis of the additional information, he agreed with Joan on the need to look for a new job.

12. BE WILLING TO ACCEPT INCOMPLETE RESOLUTION

Many couples believe that a conflict has to be completely resolved. But if both partners have fully discussed their positions, then the unresolved difficulty usually loses most of its destructive potential. The suppression, denial, displacement, and repression—characteristic of unfaced conflict—have been reduced. Consequently, anger, resentment, hostility, and aggression are less likely to occur.

Facing the conflict can build trust by making the partners real and understandable to each other. Actual resolution of the conflict is desirable, but not essential. If intimates have made their feelings known and have understood each other's view, then they can usually live more easily with the realities of their situation.

Paul and Ellen reached this point in a conflict over Paul's busy schedule. Bored by his job, but unable to get the type of work he wanted without an advanced degree, he had started taking graduate courses at the local university. Ellen objected to his spending so much time away from home, but Paul could see no solution except to quit school. He emphasized that he was going to continue, even if it meant the end of their marriage.

As he faced this important conflict, Paul revealed to Ellen the full extent of his frustration at work. She had known of his dissatisfaction, but these emotional details had not been mentioned previously. Paul also, for the first time, shared his detailed hopes for the future after obtaining his Master's Degree. Ellen still did not want him to continue with school. But now that she had a greater understanding of his feelings, she was better able to cope with his decision.

Many life situations simply don't permit both partners to be fully satisfied. But a willingness to discuss difficulties, even during times of stress, creates a better relationship.

13. CONSIDER COMPROMISE

What are the possible alternatives for change? Can you experiment with new ways of dealing with the problem and prevent old habits from interfering with the process of discovering solutions?

What are the implications of the conflict you and your partner are experiencing? Would either of you feel resentful about a change? Under what conditions would a proposed solution be acceptable? What can you do to help your intimate make a change?

At this stage both of you must consider the options and develop an acceptable solution. Compromise under these conditions should not be confused with nonconstructive bargaining. Unlike business bartering in which people try to get the best deal on goods and services, in intimate relationships one thing should not be traded for another. Rather, with a spirit of giving, determine what solution might be acceptable to both of you.

Karen and Joe found a compromise that made a big difference in their marriage. After an argument that had threatened to end in a stalemate, Karen reported:

> One of Joe's big complaints was that we never found time to go out together. Between our jobs and the kids' schedules and our separate outside activities, it was hard to find the time, we didn't want to do the same things, or there wasn't enough money. Lots of times I felt it wasn't worth it to find a babysitter, straighten the house, feed the children, and then get dressed to go out. Often it just wasn't any fun.
>
> But this time I felt maybe we could make a change if we could just get over the old hangups. I suggested we take turns making plans for weekends. Joe was pretty skeptical, but he agreed. We decided one of us would choose how to spend each weekend and would also take charge of tickets, babysitter, cash on hand, and any other arrangements that needed to be made. The other would promise to go along and try to enjoy, but not criticize. We drew straws, and Joe was first "chooser."
>
> Well, it worked. The "chooser" really felt free to choose — even to stay home if that sounded good. The other felt free to go along with any plan. We both found new things we enjoyed doing, and best of all enjoyed doing together. After several weeks we found ourselves looking forward to time together and making the choices and arrangements together. Now if we get bogged down, we laugh and ask, "Whose weekend is it?"

14. AVOID TRYING TO WIN

In order for you to win, your partner must lose. However, in an intimate fight, either you both win or you both lose. As in a nuclear disarmament agreement, if one country feels it's getting a bad deal it may sabotage or back out of the agreement and both countries will lose.

Debbie described the futility of fighting with Phil: "He always wins, so what's the use? He's verbally overpowering. I just can't manage to get my points across."

Phil proudly admitted he was more articulate than Debbie, and that he usually won the arguments. But he had lost communication, intimacy, and sexual relations with his wife. Debbie would become silent in the middle of an argument. She had lost feeling for Phil and had not had sex with him in over two years. Only after Debbie said she was leaving him did Phil agree to seek marriage counseling.

He began to realize that because of his overpowering fight tactics, Debbie was withdrawing, and they both were suffering. She was encouraged to express her feelings and ask for what she wanted. As this couple learned to deal with conflict effectively, their feelings for each other returned. They discussed issues more readily, resumed an active sex life, and regained emotional closeness.

Always trying to win reduces a relationship to a power struggle. The better objective is to find a solution that will make life together more satisfying.

INCREASING THE POSSIBILITIES FOR GROWTH

More significant than solving a single problem is learning and developing techniques for dealing with differences. As these techniques for facing conflict are applied effectively to immediate impasses, skills for solving future problems will develop and many misunderstandings will be prevented. But both cooperation and practice are required for these techniques to be most effective.

When you and your intimate feel that conflicts are being dealt with effectively, you may be ready to consider clearing out past resentments. Because sharing hurts and resentments from the past can bring out strong negative emotions, this should not be attempted unless you are both ready and willing. Intimates who decide to perform this exercise should make up a list of instances when they have been hurt by the other. By going back to any point in the relationship, resentments that have remained unmentioned may surface, and hurts that have been superficially discussed can be fully faced. It is probably best first to read all the items on each list to one another. Then thoroughly discuss one item at a time, alternating from the lists.

If you decide to attempt this exercise, allow plenty of time and be prepared to face strong emotions. The "Hurt Museum" allows you both to express painful memories and to gain understanding about these incidents. When intimates effectively deal with previously inflicted hurts, areas of oversensitivity irritated by these incidents become more manageable.

This chapter has discussed productive ways of dealing with feelings of anger and annoyance. Unfair expressions of anger—temper tantrums, nagging, uncontrolled venting, physical violence, displacement onto the wrong person, revenge that creates new problems, and overreaction to minor criticism—undermine intimacy. But in facing conflict effectively, the emphasis is on solving the problem. By admitting conflict and by disagreeing agreeably, two people can extend themselves, and both can grow. The exploration of feelings and experiences can provide more understanding of yourself, your intimate, and your relationship.

Let us share our time
yet do not give all your time
nor take all of mine
for in order to develop to the fullest
to be free
we must have solitude
and individuality.
Let me wander in solitude
when I need to be alone
yet be near
when I need you.
Let us share our love.

THOMAS S. FEE[1]

SEPARATENESS
AND
TOGETHERNESS

chapter six

QUESTIONS FROM
THE NATIONAL LOVE,
SEX & MARRIAGE TEST

Please circle the letter of the answer you think is correct.

1. The partners who have the most freedom in their relationships are those:
    - (A) who live together without being married.
    - (B) who respect the rights (freedom and privacy) of their partner.
    - (C) who are financially successful.

2. If two people trust each other, it's okay to:
    - (A) open each other's mail.
    - (B) listen in on the phone, but not open the other's mail.
    - (C) discuss what kind of privacy they want.

3. At a party, if an attractive person of the opposite sex pays a lot of attention to my mate, I would:
    - (A) have confidence in my mate.

(B) try to attract someone else, too.

(C) try to conceal my feelings.

4. If I discovered my mate had an affair with someone else, I would:

    (A) know my mate didn't love me any more.

    (B) have an affair myself.

    (C) talk about it, and work things out.

5. If my mate has a hobby that I don't care for, it is best:

    (A) to do it, too, even if I don't like it.

    (B) for my mate to do something else we both can enjoy.

    (C) for each of us to give in a little.

The following are the correct answers.

1. **The Correct Answer Is: (B)**
Freedom cannot be measured objectively. No adult has the inherent right to control another, married or not. What constitutes restraints in one relationship may not in another. It's how the two people define the relationship that determines how free each of the partners is. Each couple must define (decide) on what types of freedoms they desire and will accept.

2. **The Correct Answer Is: (C)**
A person cannot *assume* that some act is acceptable to one's partner without "checking it out." Just because Ma and Pa did it this way doesn't mean it's going to work in your relationship. Again, communication, discussion, and a willingness to compromise are the bases for an intimate, loving relationship.

3. **The Correct Answer Is: (A)**
Trying to "get even" with a partner for behavior of which you do not approve rarely does anything other than escalate the hostility of the other persons involved. On the other hand, trying to conceal one's true feelings is not usually productive behavior, either. Having feel-

ings is always all right. People get into trouble, however, for handling their feelings through ineffective
behavior. If you answered that you would have confidence in your mate, you are probably better as a
partner.

4. **The Correct Answer Is: (C)**
   No matter how painful it may seem, trying to work
   things out is a better solution than jumping to the
   conclusion that your mate doesn't love you ... and
   certainly better than retaliation by having an affair,
   too. In fact, if one wishes to hold a relationship together,
   the latter is unfair to the object of the affair, too.

5. **The Correct Answer Is: (C)**
   Even if it is not the ideal solution for either person, a
   compromise that works is better than having a "win-
   ner" and a "loser," even over what to do with leisure
   time. Demanding that a partner do something you both
   enjoy when the hobby is a true pleasure is likely to
   result in resentment whether it is expressed or not
   (better get a hobby of your own!).[2]

A national sample of 461 single and 565 married
people answered about four of these five questions correctly.
More difficult than the answering of five questions is the
act of balancing separateness and togetherness in everyday
life. Intimacy requires a dynamic, changing balance between
separateness and togetherness. Neither the cult of arrogant
individualism nor the opposite—being together all the time
and having only shared interests—will work. Both can be
forms of tyranny which undermine a relationship.

You can achieve greater freedom, or greater closeness, or both, if you discuss what you want for yourself ("I")
and what you both want for your relationship ("We"). Although a final solution can never be reached because of
inevitable differences and because you, your intimate, and

your relationship are always changing, facing the issues keeps separateness and togetherness in better balance.

What do you want for yourself? Listed below are some areas requiring "I" decisions.

- Career
- Self-development goals
- Dress
- Physical appearance
- Friendships
- Leisure time
- Hobbies
- Time to be alone
- Private physical space (even in your own home)
- What you will not share

When you make "I" decisions you take responsibility, but your "I" decisions often produce "We" effects and therefore influence your relationship.

What do you want for your relationship ("We")? What do you both expect in the following areas?

- Communication
- Household maintenance
- Parenting
- Sexual activities
- Time together
- Activities together
- Common goals and values
- Money management
- Amount of flexibility in roles
- Amount of time spent with parents and relatives

- Amount of time spent with other couples
- Willingness to encourage each other's individual development

Merle Shain writes:

Loving someone means helping them to be more them-selves, which can be different from being what you'd like them to be, although often they turn out the same. When you ask someone to live through you and for you, they warp like a Japanese tree to suit the relationship which you are, and cease to be what you chose them for, that is, cease to be themselves. So men who are loving like as much as they love, and somehow they find the courage to let their partners grow in the direction they need to grow, even if that contains the risk that they might grow away.

Good people can't be possessed and those who can one never wants for long. No one gives you security—you have to do that for yourself.[3]

Couples who attempt to find security through total togetherness create problems for themselves. Possessive lovers may try to be the sole source of joy and security for each other, but they never can succeed at this impossible task. Intimates cannot be all things to each other.

The intimate of a possessive lover may initially enjoy the togetherness and the attention. One man, who at first liked the almost constant togetherness that he and his wife experienced, later complained that the only time he could get any privacy at home was when he locked himself in the bathroom with the newspaper. Betty, a 23-year-old woman, at first enjoyed all the attention she received from her possessive lover. During their four months of dating, he always had lunch with her, called her several times a day, and met her after work so that she could never go for a drink with her girlfriends. Now that they have been married a year, he continues these activities and also listens in on her telephone conversations at home. She still likes all the attention, but she misses spending time with friends and she often argues with him about her refusal to succumb to his demand that she stop working.

Too much separateness, like too much togetherness, can also cause problems in an intimate relationship. A cult of autonomy—independence carried to the extreme—has become fashionable in some circles in recent years. The "You do your thing, I do my thing; no questions asked or promises made" philosophy enhances isolation and loneliness because one partner has little impact on the other. A 37-year-old divorced woman reflected on a just-terminated relationship with a lover who preached the freedom philosophy.

> I was involved with someone who had the Fritz Perls "You each do your own thing" poster on his wall. This sounded beautiful in theory, but it didn't actually work very well in practice. In our relationship it usually worked out that he did his thing and I did his thing, too, because the relationship was more important to me than it was to him. There were absolutely no commitments and I spent a year filled with broken dates, constantly changing plans, and insecurity. I tried to convince myself that a totally free "do your own thing" type of relationship was somehow preferable to the old-style relationship in which you could usually be reasonably certain of seeing someone on Saturday night. Perhaps he really needed that much freedom—perhaps he didn't really care—perhaps he was afraid of becoming vulnerable if he made any commitments. I didn't need total freedom and didn't take advantage of having it.
>
> Perhaps this "do your own thing" type of relationship can

work well between two people who care equally, but if one is more powerful than the other, the weaker person seems to be in danger of being exploited. The needs of two individuals will probably never balance completely. What happens on the night when one individual has a very strong need to be alone and his partner has an equally strong need to be with him? Some form of compromise is obviously necessary or one partner is bound to feel cheated. If the same partner is continually cheated, the relationship takes more from him than it gives.

I don't mean to imply that it's wrong to try to see that our own needs are met, just that by entering into a relationship—any relationship—we give up some of our personal freedom for the sake of the relationship. If I answer my telephone, I am choosing to relate on some level to whomever is calling rather than to be absolutely free to do whatever I please. I'm willing to relinquish some of my freedom to experience the joys that a good relationship can provide. To me, a relationship in which each partner is continually "doing his own thing" ceases to be definable as a relationship.

I think many people brought up with the idea that marriage lasts forever are so afraid of becoming trapped in a bad marriage that they are hesitant to make even short-term commitments for fear of accidently becoming more involved than they want to be. Feeling responsible for another individual often breeds resentment, but feeling needed by another if his needs are neither unrealistic nor excessive often promotes intimacy.

A large amount of separateness occurs and may create problems when one of the partners has a job requiring much travel or has commitments requiring much time and energy. Many highly productive or highly creative people put their energy into their work with little left over for their partners. An extreme example was Mahatma Gandhi, famous for his devotion to India. He said he needed his total energy for working on national problems and he renounced sexual intercourse early in his marriage. Not surprisingly, the biographies of creative geniuses often show much marital discord.[4]

TIME

Some couples want much time together, some couples want much time apart, and some couples vacillate because of changing wants and needs. As partners go through different stages, outside time demands will change. And some types of outside activities will be more acceptable than others. For example, partners usually show more tolerance for outside activities that will benefit both of them—such as one of the intimates going to school to improve occupational potential—than they do for separate recreational or social activities. But each couple has to decide for themselves.

Even when a couple wants more time together, demands from children, family, friends, jobs, meetings, and everyday activities may provide obstacles. Many people get caught in the trap of taking on too many responsibilities. One simple solution is to learn how to say "no" to some of the time-consuming activity. Another option might be to schedule periods when just the two of you will be together.

A simple exercise you might try involves each of you making three lists. The first list consists of activities you liked to do together in the past. The second list consists of things you always wanted to do but never got around to doing. For the third list write down activities you do now that you would like to do more often.[5] By sharing the lists with your partner, you may learn better ways of spending your time together. The quality of activities together is often more important than the quantity.

Many parents have difficulty finding time to be together without the children. Yet most couples enjoy time away from their children, even if it is in their own home. A 34-year-old woman confronted this problem.

> One of our few major problems was a lack of privacy. I'm a loud lover. Since we have three kids, we found it difficult to get the house totally to ourselves. We had a meeting of the minds and came up with this solution. We now put a Santa Claus on the front door. This tells the kids, and anyone who knows us well, to go away and stay away until the Santa is removed. During November and December we change to a Halloween pumpkin. It has worked out very well.

Other ways to be together without the children include taking them to the movies, arranging "trades" with friends and neighbors, and getting a babysitter.

RE-ENTRY PROBLEMS

Jane, a 32-year-old woman, observed:

> When Fred would go out of town on a business trip for several days I would miss him terribly. But then when he'd come home, no matter how glad we acted about seeing each other, I felt like he was a stranger to me. The separation had caused distance between us and we needed time to fill the gap. I would look forward to sex because I thought then we would be "together" again. This worked sometimes, but other times I was so tense and so un-

myself that by the time we got into bed I couldn't enjoy sex with him. I would feel empty and experience a sense of loss. This just made me feel even more distant from him and also angry that he hadn't satisfied my need to be close to him again. Sometimes he would be tense too and wouldn't be able to get an erection. Finally we began talking about this and realized that we needed to get to know each other again a little before we had sex.

Now when he comes home we are both aware that the time away has created psychological distance between us and we spend time talking and sharing each other first— I guess you could say we spend some time "mind-fucking" first. Now that this is all out in the open and we don't demand instant closeness from each other the minute he steps in the door, we're finding that it takes much less time to "bridge the gap" again. And now we find enjoyment in the little moments that we feel we're back together again—something as little as getting a glass of milk out of the refrigerator together and laughing over little things makes us realize that we're both at home again.

Getting back together again, even after a brief separation, causes anxiety. This anxiety may result in excitement or tension or both. As Jane and Fred discovered, the best way to re-enter each other's lives is to go through a reintroduction. Whether the couple is dating or is married the same principle applies—re-establish your specific togetherness as intimates.

JEALOUSY

The word "jealousy" evokes a wide variety of images and associations. Shakespeare called jealousy "the green-eyed

monster." Milton called it "the injured lover's hell." To
Dryden it was "the jaundice of the soul." These definitions
are as relevant in our society today as they were when first
written.

Anthropologists have not been able to find a society
completely free of jealousy, but what will cause jealousy
does vary tremendously from culture to culture. California
psychologist Ralph Hupka provides the following fabricated
vignette to illustrate how different cultures prescribe different cues for triggering a jealousy evaluation:

> The event takes place in a primitive society of approxi-
> mately 100 members. On her return trip from the local
> watering well a married woman is asked for a cup of
> water by a male resident of the village. Her husband,
> resting on the porch of their dwelling, observes his wife
> giving the man a cup of water. Subsequently, they ap-
> proach the husband and the three of them enjoy a lively
> and friendly conversation into the late evening hours.
> Eventually the husband puts out the lamp, and the guest
> has sexual intercourse with the wife. The next morning
> the husband leaves the house early in order to catch fishes
> for breakfast. Upon his return he finds his wife having
> sex again with the guest. The husband becomes violently
> enraged and mortally stabs the guest.

> At what point in the vignette may one expect the husband
> to be jealous? It depends, of course, in which culture we
> place the husband. A husband of the Yurok Indian tribe of
> California in the 19th century challenged any man to a
> fight who dared to request a cup of water from his wife.
> An Ammassalik Eskimo husband, on the other hand,
> offered his wife to a guest by means of the culturally
> sanctioned game of "Putting out the lamp." A good host
> was expected to turn out the lamp at night. This was an
> invitation for the guest to have sexual intercourse with
> the wife. The Ammassalik, however, became intensely

jealous when his wife copulated with a guest in circumstances other than the lamp game or without a mutual agreement between two families to exchange mates. It was not unusual for the husband to kill the interloper.

The Toda of Southern India, who were primarily polyandrous at the turn of the century, . . . would consider the sequence of events described in the vignette to be perfectly normal. That is to say, the husband would not have been upset to find his wife having sexual relations again in the morning if the man were her *mokhthodvaiol*. The Todas had the custom of *mokhthoditi* which allowed husbands and wives to take on lovers. When, for instance, a man wanted someone else's wife as a lover he sought the consent of the wife and her husband or husbands. If consent was given by all, the men negotiated for the annual fee to be received by the husband(s). The woman then lived with the man just as if she were his real wife. Or, more commonly, the man visited the woman at the house of her husband(s).

It is evident from these illustrations that the culture, far more than the individual, determines when one is to recognize threat and to experience stress. Events have meaning only in the context of the culture.[6]

Our culture sanctions jealousy and often views it as a measure of love. Our society perpetuates a romantic philosophy for love and marriage, fosters the myth of a perfect intimate relationship, and therefore increases our susceptibility to jealousy. Moreover, in a society placing much value on ownership and private property, people become more possessive of both things and people. Any adherence to the concept of a mate's being one's property further encourages jealousy.

In American society today, men and women deal with jealous feelings differently.

Men are more apt to *deny* jealous feelings; women are more apt to *acknowledge* them. Men are more likely than women to express jealous feelings through rage and even violence, but such outbursts are often followed by despondency. Jealous men are more apt to focus on the outside *sexual* activity of the partner and they often demand a recital of the intimate details; jealous women are more likely to focus on the *emotional* involvement between [their] partner and the third party. Men are more likely to *externalize* the cause of the jealousy, more likely to blame the partner, or the third party, or "circumstances." Women often *internalize* the cause of jealousy; they blame themselves. Similarly, a jealous man is more likely to display *competitive* behavior toward the third party while a jealous woman is more likely to display *possessive* behavior. She clings to her partner rather than confronting the third party.[7]

For both men and women, jealousy can be elicited in many different ways. The following newspaper article describes an event that elicited jealousy from many people. How would you and your intimate have reacted in a similar situation?

Honest, honey—it's all a mistake

CHICAGO (AP)—Hundreds of surprised spouses found themselves with some explaining to do after a mailing foulup by a computer firm sent them letters thanking them for staying recently at a downtown hotel.

A letter intended for regular guests of the Oxford House, a Chicago hotel, was sent in error to about 4,000 city and suburban residents because the wrong computer tape was used to produce the letters.

It wasn't long before the switchboard at the Oxford House

lit up with about 500 phone calls from husbands and wives suspicious of extramarital activity.

"One woman whose name was on the letter had three children and was pregnant with a fourth," said Jerome Belanger, hotel vice president and general manager. "She said her husband was mad and doubted the child was his."

The letter, announcing renovations at the hotel, included each recipient's name in the greeting and in one paragraph. The message, which arrived with Wednesday's mail, began, "Being privileged in having you as our recent guest . . .

Belanger said one woman called in tears and begged, "Please explain to my husband that I was not a guest there."

"I was amazed at some of the calls," Belanger said.

One woman who had begun divorce proceedings was upset to find the letter was a mistake. "She said she hoped to use the letter against her husband," Belanger said.

All who received the Oxford House letter will be mailed retraction notices by the computer firm, Compuletter Inc. Gary Ross, company president, said a random tape for sample mailings to areas southwest of the Loop was inadvertently fed through the computers.

Belanger said the whole incident just may go to show "husbands and wives don't trust each other much these days."[8]

Even when there is trust, such a letter is likely to raise questions in a partner's mind. Virtually every man and every woman at some point experiences jealousy. For many people, jealousy turns into a green-eyed monster. How can the monster be tamed? The first step is to admit the jealous feelings. The next is to determine whether the perceived threat is real. Gwen, a 30-year-old mother of two children, discovered that the monster existed only in her mind.

> I have learned through experience that jealousy is just a waste of good energy. Several years ago my husband mentioned that a young woman in Massachusetts had been writing him and wanted to come study pottery with him. I thought that was nice but wondered why the correspondence from this mysterious person continued over several months. Feeling insecure about our relationship at that time in my life and feeling an extended form of postpartum depression, I fantasized the entire affair that my husband would have with this person once she arrived in town. As the day grew closer I grew more and more anxious and was literally mesmerized when my husband asked me if I would pick her up at the airport. Of course I had never told my husband of these imagined fears on my part, so I readily agreed to pick up "his new friend." As I stood at the gate I really had to brace myself while I waited for her. I had no idea what she looked like or anything about her. Soon a very shy but friendly young woman walked through the gate and I knew immediately that this was her. We both looked at each other and it was like falling in love at first sight. Our rapport was incredible and to this day we are best friends. I often laugh when I think of how I let this jealousy (fear of the unknown) eat me up for weeks. I realized what an enemy the mind can be if we let it run rampant.

When Gwen discovered that no threat existed, the monster quickly disappeared. But why did the monster stay around as long as it did? One part of the answer is because Gwen and her husband had not discussed the problem. And the other part follows a general rule—the worse a person feels about himself and the less secure he feels in his relationship, the more the susceptibility to jealousy.

Talking about jealousy with your intimate usually helps. Exactly what do you expect from each other? Which types of behaviors with members of the opposite sex are acceptable? Which are taboo? What is bothering you now? Be as specific as possible about what is making you jealous.

Family therapist Larry Constantine lists six situations that can cause jealousy in a relationship:

1. Loss of face, status, or ego-enhancement.
2. Loss of need gratification, including sexual, intellectual, emotional, and other needs.
3. Loss of control over one's partner, of control of one's own life, of power in relation to one's partner.
4. Loss of predictability, the dependability of one's partner's behavior.
5. Loss of privacy, territory, or exclusive access.
6. Loss of actual time with one's partner, or reduced contact.[9]

Identifying the specific cause of your annoyance and getting in touch with your feelings is important in managing jealousy. It enables you to discuss the issue more effectively with your intimate. But good communication, even though it usually reduces jealousy, does not always solve the problem. Sometimes a compromise is needed.

Margaret had been dating Phil a month when he told her not to visit with her friends unless he was with her. Margaret refused. Looking back, she recalls:

I told him he couldn't own me or control me, but that I would be open and honest with him. I told Phil that deception leads to jealousy, and that I was going to be honest, monogamous, and independent. I reassured him of my commitment to him, but also said that I just had to be

myself and do my own thing. When Phil finally learned
that I was not a sneak, that I cared for him and that I was
going to keep my necessary independence he accepted me.

Even people who consider themselves sexually liberated experience jealousy, although many of these people
feel guilty about being jealous. In a *Village Voice* article,
Karen Durbin provided a telling description of this problem
and concluded that sexual jealousy has become the new sin
of the liberated generation. She says that all jealousy is a
cry of pain, and to ignore, suppress, or condemn it is at best
unhelpful, at worst cruel. She predicts that sexual jealousy
will probably be a human problem as long as sex remains
an expression of love and as long as love remains an effective
means, apart from religion, of assuaging our essential
isolation.[10]

Once upon a time there was a little fish who was a bird from the waist up and who was madly in love with a little bird who was a fish from the waist up. So the Fish-Bird kept saying to the Bird-Fish: "Oh, why were we created so that we can never live together? You in the wind and I in the wave. What a pity for both of us." And the Bird-Fish would answer: "No, what luck for both of us. This way we'll always be in love because we'll always be separated."

VASSILIS VASSILIKOS[1]

MAKING THE LOVE LAST

chapter seven

Maintaining a love relationship over a long period of time is difficult. Recall Erich Fromm's observation, quoted in the Introduction: "There is hardly any activity, any enterprise, which is started with such tremendous hopes and expectations and yet which fails so regularly as love." The high divorce rate in the United States is just one indication of the extent to which lovers are regularly experiencing such failures.

What can be done to make the love last? To what do couples who have remained happy attribute their success? Here are some answers from those who consider themselves to be happily married:

> Walter and I have been married for six years. Our marriage has been bliss. We have had our blisters from time to time, but each time we heal and the blisters have become less and less frequent. We have a tremendous amount of love and respect for one another. We are also intelligent and have enough common sense to talk things out and try to help one another.
>
> I'm a great believer in "you can solve the problem, if you know what the problem is." Being able to communicate certainly is the key to happiness. Let me add that Walter

and I are not perfect people; therefore, we do not have a perfect marriage. We do have a happy marriage. To use a simile, our marriage is like a swing. We hit our highs and lows. Sometimes we fall off and skin our knees. But, it's so much fun, we get right back on, put forth a little effort, and before you know it we're hitting that happy high again!

She: I am happily married because there is someone to share successes and failures. Someone who I can always be myself around, even at my ugliest moments, who will love me after all is said and done. He is my very best friend—I can bare my soul and he is there to give me whatever support I need.

Through the trials and struggles of our marriage, and there have been many in our ten years, I have grown more in love with him after each struggle. We have grown together in love and spirit and will continue to grow as the struggles of life continue. But, the best feeling is knowing no matter what happens to me, I can turn around and gather sustaining strength from the man I married— the man who loves me.

Our society has forgotten one of the greatest gifts in this world—Love. To love and be loved is all that makes us what we are.

He: I am a happily married man of almost ten years. In those ten years, I have had to do many things that many men would not or will not do, and that is to listen to my wife. I don't mean the kind of listening when she says to take out the garbage, I mean the listening that allows me to understand how she feels, where she is coming from. How can I love her completely without knowing her?

I have had to also give myself to her in the same way. We have to share feelings, moods, excitements, and disappointments together to achieve the kind of relationship a marriage is supposed to have.

I guess the main thing my wife and I have is a commitment toward each other and our family. We are committed to marriage, we know it will work because we work at it. It is ours, and no one can take it from us. She is also my very best friend.

We discussed the reasons we have succeeded in love where so many have failed. Our "secret," if you want to call it that, boils down to two things. First, we recognize that marriage is a partnership, and that a partnership is a difficult relationship to sustain. Why? Because there are two bosses. This means that both people must be willing to sacrifice and to compromise to the extent necessary to keep the overall relationship flourishing. Neither can have his or her way all the time—both will lose a certain amount of personal freedom or flexibility.

Second, we talk to each other; about anything and every-thing—something I read, something she saw, a new idea, an old memory. It doesn't matter what; we just keep in touch.

We've changed a lot in our ten years of togetherness. But we strongly feel that, in a world that has grown so cold and impersonal, there is a definite need to have a "home base" where you know you will be secure, respected, and loved. Therefore each of us tries to be supportive of the other in the family. I could go on and on; I'm so proud of this family.

We have been married twelve years and are very happy. We have given this much thought and feel it is due to total commitment to a successful relationship. We use the word relationship because it is the key word. The insti-tution of marriage may or may not survive, but people will always need and seek interpersonal relationships.

We have disagreements, and we feel some amount of disagreement could even be considered healthy, because a bland marriage is like a bland diet. Emotions should be kept strong and viable. At the same time, marriage should also bring the comfort and ease of old friendships. Marriage can and should contain the elements of both an affair and a family.

Life is a process of growth and change. We have grown and changed together. We have given each other space to grow. We have shared our growth. We have pooled our experiences and knowledge and actually have a better meeting of the minds over time. We discuss, acknowledge, and accept our differences.

Food is necessary to keep anything alive. We nurture our love and relationship so that it will be a happy one.

My real life began in 1963 when at the age of 28 I met Mary. There were times before my marriage when I seriously wondered if I would ever find that person with whom I would share my life completely.

Never have I regretted the commitment I made to Mary. We share countless interests in common—music, art, literature, church, travel—not to mention our greatest cooperative venture, our children. They provide a never-ending supply of energy and enthusiasm, frustration and exasperation, delightful discovery, and joyous pride—but most of all our marriage means a sharing of each other physically, mentally, emotionally, spiritually. I'm not suggesting that everything has been perfect. If I made such an unrealistic claim about marital bliss I'd be lying. There have been many upsets, a lot of misunderstandings, and more than a few serious arguments, but no such encounter has ever occurred without being followed by a significant growth in our mutual love, understanding, and sensitivity to each other's feelings and needs.

We will celebrate our twenty-fifth wedding anniversary next year. There has never been any serious thought about separation, because when we married, it was for eternity. We were mature enough to look at a goal outside ourselves. Our number one goal was, and is now, to follow the will of God for our lives. We have had God as our outside source of strength during illness and disappointments. We have had our love for each other to motivate each to think of the other's needs first. So many persons today think only of what makes *me* happy.

What makes us know we are happy? That listening ear when things have gone wrong at the office; that gentle tease when we need a sense of humor; the sharing of the birth of two healthy babies; helping them grow to well-adjusted young adulthood; sharing our lives and philosophy with people around us. We don't smother each other, but we know we have a commitment. We have tried not to let our lives be centered around material things. We enjoy our comforts, but these are not at the center of our relationship. These are only tools to be used in our relationship with others. We know we are not perfect, but by reinforcing the positive in each of us, we have worked toward the ultimate in this relationship known as marriage.

In the past at least, marriage has been the model for most long-term love relationships. Therefore, using the term "happily married" to describe a long, successful intimate relationship is more an acceptance of reality as it exists today than a value judgment that marriage is the way. Two people achieving their objectives in a love relationship is what is most important.

An increasing number of couples are deciding to live together, but the objective is usually a temporary rather than a long-term arrangement. Between 1970 and 1976, the number of unmarried couples living together doubled.[2] In her "Review of Research on Nonmarital Cohabitation in the United States," Eleanor Macklin observed that cohabitation relationships are in many ways very similar to noncohabitation relationships. She concluded that only a very small percentage of those living together will choose cohabitation over marriage as a permanent lifestyle. The social, economic, and legal benefits for marriage continue to be very strong. But the increased popularity of living together will probably be accompanied by a gradual increase in permissiveness and experimentation within the marital relationship itself.[3]

Attacking marriage is now fashionable. "Marriage is a great institution, but who wants to live in an institution?" goes one joke. Yet if the concept of marriage were unknown and were being proposed for the first time, it would be greeted as a clever idea. A committed relationship between a man and a woman can meet many fundamental needs and can generate feelings of happiness, worth, and fulfillment. The concept of marriage, if viewed as the creative sharing of life, has much potential. But neither marriage nor other forms of intimate man–woman relationships are living up to their potential. Marriage merely serves as a scapegoat for the problems that pervade man–woman intimacy.

One problem in making the love last is balancing security and excitement. People want intimates who will be understanding and dependable, but they also want excitement and novelty. In time, partners usually provide more security and less excitement.[4] The boredom experienced by so many married couples is parodied by the image of the middle-aged married couple sitting silently in a restaurant. But boredom is not limited to marital relationships. A study of 103 couples who had broken up before marriage revealed that "becoming bored with the relationship" was the most frequent complaint among both the men and the women.[5]

Variety is an effective way of attacking boredom. Love is too often taken for granted, and would increase greatly if people would spend as much time on their relationships as they spend on their lawns. Creativity, spontaneity, imagination, and flexibility can provide new opportunities for experiencing one another in different ways.

ADDING VARIETY TO YOUR RELATIONSHIP

Some couples say that a disadvantage of being together for a long time is that there is nothing new to learn about each other. This is simply not true. Partners can, of course, fall into the rut of taking each other for granted and following a stagnant routine. But the opportunity to explore a familiar person in new ways is always there. People who are interested in each other will always have new things they can learn about one another. Unfortunately, many partners become so preoccupied with jobs, children, household maintenance, and other tasks of daily living that they end up relating in a stereotyped, routine manner.

The following sentence completion exercise can help you and your partner learn new things about each other.[6] The twenty-five sentences can be completed either verbally or in writing.

1. What I like best about our sex life is . . .
2. What I like least about our sex life is . . .
3. Love is . . .
4. Recently, I have daydreamed about . . .
5. During the next ten years I hope to . . .
6. I secretly fear . . .
7. I secretly hope . . .
8. I am ashamed of . . .

9. I am proud of ...
10. I would like to develop an interest in ...
11. I wish you were interested in ...
12. I wish we would talk more about ...
13. This past year I discovered that you ...
14. I admire people who ...
15. I cannot understand why some people ...
16. To me, money ...
17. Religious people are ...
18. My concept of religion is ...
19. My concept of what happens to a person after death is
    ...
20. The three parts of my body I like most are ...
21. The three parts of my body I like least are ...
22. The parts of your body I like most are ...
23. When I first met you, I ...
24. I feel good when you say ...
25. If I could magically have three wishes fulfilled, they
    would be ...

Surprise Your Partner With An "I Appreciate" List. A graduate student in psychology sent the following letter to his girlfriend, who at the time was living in another state and was experiencing much stress from her new job.

Dearest Janet,

I love you very much and I appreciate you very much, and I always will. I want to let you know some of the ways I appreciate you and have appreciated you. I appreciate:

1. that you are the only person in the whole world I can trust 100% completely

2. *what a wonderful friend you are*
3. *what a great love you are*
4. *your love*
5. *that you are by far the closest family I now have*
6. *how we can assume so many different roles together*
7. *how I can truly be myself with you*
8. *your enthusiasm for life and small things*
9. *the beautiful Valentine's Day poem you sent me*
10. *the peak rainy Sundays together*
11. *how extremely well you perceive my uniqueness*
12. *holding your hand*
13. *making love with you*
14. *your passion*
15. *holding you before we fall asleep*
16. *sleeping next to you*
17. *waking up next to you and holding you in the morning*
18. *your sparkling eyes which are so alive*
19. *your super-sexy massages*
20. *the softness of your skin*
21. *the sexy feel of your breasts while making love*
22. *your sexy hands*
23. *your touch*
24. *your spunk*
25. *your patience with me*
26. *your understanding*
27. *your warmth*
28. *your perceptiveness*
29. *your spirituality*
30. *reading in bed with you*

31. *your intelligence*

32. *your tremendous feel for people*

33. *how much everyone I know likes you*

34. *how much I rely on your judgment and advice*

35. *how you think I'm more spiritual than you even though you're more spiritual than I am*

36. *how I really feel appreciated by you*

37. *how you affirm what I am and what I want to be*

38. *how you have shown me that honesty in a relationship can really work*

39. *our trip to Houston and your being my only girlfriend who has met my mother*

40. *our trip to N.Y.*

41. *our trip to Fort Walton Beach*

42. *your coming through when I've been down or in crisis and have needed you*

43. *our first trip to Atlanta*

44. *our many fantastic dinners together with the understanding and being together flowing*

45. *your encouragement*

46. *the sense of security which you alone give me*

47. *all the super-sexy erotic thoughts I've had about you since I've known you*

48. *how very giving you are*

49. *your sense of humor*

50. *your laugh*

51. *your integrity*

52. *our holidays together*

53. *our meditations together*

54. *your touching poems*

This is just a partial list. I can go on, but I have to mail

this now so that you'll receive it by Tues.
I love you.

Wayne

Blind Walk. Blindfold your partner and go for a ten-minute walk together. Make the experience more interesting by walking over different surfaces and by having your partner touch different objects. After the ten minutes, immediately reverse roles. When you have both completed the walk, discuss how you each felt during the experience.

A List of My Needs, Your Needs, and Our Needs.[7] First make a list of what you think you need to be happy. Then make a list of what you think your intimate needs to be happy. And finally, compose a list of what you think the relationship needs to make it a good one. After finishing the lists, share and discuss them with each other.

A relationship is most likely to satisfy the needs of both partners if each says what he or she wants from the relationship. To discuss what you want for your *self* is not being selfish— it is a path to mutual growth.

Your Statue.[8] Think about what type of statue you would make to depict your relationship. Then silently pose your partner in the right position. Make sure your partner's pose and facial expression are the way you want them to be. Then pose yourself as part of the sculpture, and hold the pose for one minute. After that, reverse roles and repeat the experience.

Afterward, discuss what your statues represented.

Fantasy Associations. Think about what type of animal, flower, vegetable, or car your partner reminds you of and then share these ideas with your partner.

Give Your Partner a Coupon Book. You can give your intimate coupons as a gift. For instance, one coupon could be for going to a special place, another for an activity you normally don't like to do, another for breakfast in bed. You can also specify when your intimate can use the coupons (" only on Sunday," or "only after 10 A.M."). The coupons are best when they are personal and specific to your relationship.

An Overview of Variety and Surprise. The previous suggestions give a glimpse at how intimates can experience one another in new ways. The possibilities are infinite. If you are willing to think about surprising your intimate and if you are willing to use your imagination, new avenues for variety and excitement open up.

Overcoming Sexual Problems

After some couples have been together for some time, sex, like going to parties, is not as much fun as it's supposed to be. Imaginative couples, however, can add stimulating variety to their sexual repertoire and can maintain a good part of the excitement while at the same time enjoying the comfort of familiarity. A balance between surprise and predictability makes for good sex.

Over time, an effort must be made to keep the surprise part from diminishing. The quest for variety, however, should not turn into a total preoccupation with technique. Sex was never meant to be a competitive sport. A focus on performance, rather than on enjoyment and variety and closeness, leads to problems and unrealistic expectations.

In general, people expect too much from sex. As with

other areas of life, perfection is unattainable. In the course of a lifetime, every man is going to experience times when he is unable to get an erection and every woman is going to experience times when she is sexually unarousable. And sex is certainly not the panacea to solve difficulties in other areas of the relationship. One woman in marriage counseling complained, "If I'm depressed or upset, he thinks a good screw will solve the problem." Although good sex cannot solve the problems in other areas of a relationship, the elimination of sexual problems can greatly help a relationship.

The most common sexual problem in men is premature ejaculation. Sex therapists William Masters and Virginia Johnson estimate that millions of men are affected by it.[9] Yet a relatively simple technique can solve the problem almost 98 percent of the time if there is good verbal communication between the partners. A description of the squeeze technique for the treatment of premature ejaculation follows.

When a man achieves an erection, the woman can use the " squeeze technique." She places her thumb on the underside of the penis (just where the shaft and the head of the penis meet), and she places two fingers on the other side of the penis, one finger on each side of the ridge that separates the head from the shaft. She then squeezes her thumb and first two fingers together for about four seconds. The squeeze should be sufficiently hard to cause the man to lose some of his erection. He will also lose the urge to ejaculate. After about twenty seconds, the woman should manipulate her partner to full erection once more. At the appropriate time, the squeeze is again used to prevent ejaculation. The squeeze technique may be applied up to five times for a given session.

At first, the squeeze technique can be used during sexual intercourse with the woman on top. If the man is close to ejaculation, the woman raises her body, uses the squeeze technique, and then shortly thereafter reinserts the penis. Another way of supplementing the squeeze technique is for the man and woman to stop movement for about thirty seconds when the man is close to ejaculation.

As ejaculatory control increases, other positions of sexual intercourse can be tried. When the problem of premature ejaculation has been solved, the couple should still use the squeeze technique at least once a week for at least six months. Premature ejaculation is the easiest sexual problem to treat, and Masters and Johnson believe that it could be virtually eliminated if their technique were fully known and used.

A much more complex situation occurs with women who find it difficult to achieve orgasm. A full treatment of this problem is beyond the scope of this book; some suggestions, however, will be made.

The most important suggestion involves exercises originally designed by a professor of gynecology, Dr. Arnold Kegel, to cure urinary incontinence. These exercises, by strengthening the pubococcygeus muscle, can also help a woman reach orgasm. A growing number of sex therapists and gynecologists are adding Kegel exercises to the treatment program for orgasmic problems; and in addition, as a technique for making good lovemaking even better.

The first step in doing these exercises is to identify the pubococcygeus muscle. By sitting on a toilet with legs spread as far apart as possible and by starting and stopping urination, a woman can identify this muscle.

One exercise is to contract the pubococcygeus muscle, hold for three seconds, and then relax it and repeat the process. At least sixty contractions a day are recommended. (But remember that any muscle that is exercised more than usual may at first become sore, so a gradual buildup may be necessary.) The more this muscle is exercised, the stronger it will become. Another exercise is to release and contract the pubococcygeus muscle very rapidly ten times in succession. This can be done up to thirty times a day. This flicking action somewhat approximates what the pubococcygeus muscle does involuntarily during orgasm.

A method for promoting orgasm during sexual intercourse is manual stimulation of the genital area. Either the man or the woman can actively touch and stimulate the clitoral area during intercourse.

In general, the more intimates help each other to overcome sexual difficulties and the more they open themselves up to one another, the more their potential for mutual enjoyment. Think of the limitless possibilities for sexual enjoyment in terms of time, method, and place. Become more aware of the sexual potential between you and your intimate.

SEVEN INGREDIENTS FOR MAKING THE LOVE LAST

What makes some relationships satisfying, enriching, growth-producing, and maybe even permanent? I have interviewed couples with good relationships, have read letters from people who consider themselves happily married, and have studied books, articles, and research on what makes a relationship work. Although the mystery of love may never be fully explained, there are some common threads running through good relationships, and I offer my conclusions on what makes love last. You have to form your own opinions based on *your* experiences, current situation, and future hopes.

A relationship can be successful without all the components being fully present. Much like a superb recipe, if one or two ingredients are underrepresented, the result may still be good, even though short of its ideal potential. In general, the greater the percentage of the following ingredients, the better the relationship. The ingredients for making the love last are as follows:

1. Self-acceptance and personal growth
2. Good communication
3. Ability to face conflict effectively
4. Realistic expectations
5. Commitment
6. Shared dreams and/or interests
7. Appreciation of each other

1. SELF-ACCEPTANCE AND PERSONAL GROWTH

In chapter 3 we discussed becoming intimate with yourself. As one man said, "Marriage for us didn't happen out of boredom or fear or loneliness. We liked our single lives, but decided to build a richer life together. Many relationships fail because the people basically don't love themselves and therefore can't love anyone else. In our marriage, we give to each other the same love and respect we have for ourselves."

The more parts of yourself you accept, the more you will accept and understand your intimate. Mutual self-acceptance promotes personal growth for both the individuals and the relationship.

2. GOOD COMMUNICATION

The need for good communication is an important thread running throughout this entire book. Communication is an important key to making the relationship last.

3. ABILITY TO FACE CONFLICT EFFECTIVELY

Couples in lasting relationships usually tackle crises, rather than avoid them. Chapter 6 discussed facing conflict effectively.

4. REALISTIC EXPECTATIONS

Our society fosters unrealistic romantic expectations and propagates the myth that everything will somehow work out if you are in love. Erotic lovers, particularly prone to fall into this romantic trap, often think that love will conquer all. But even in the best relationships, the partners fall short of reaching many of their hopes and expectations.

A much lower level of expectation is apparent in the philosophy of a woman who said,"I am married. Am I truly happily married? The answer is no. I have had moments of great happiness but I have also had moments of great unhappiness. Do I want a divorce? Absolutely not. The grass is the same —only the pasture is different."

5. COMMITMENT

Intimates who are committed to working together on their changing and evolving relationship have the best chance of maintaining their love and their growth. Every relationship will encounter some difficult times. When intimates face and successfully deal with the inevitable crises, feelings of commitment, trust, and security increase. Ideally, there should be a commitment to yourself, to your intimate, and to your relationship.

"The only place where success comes before work is in the dictionary," said a 31-year-old man. "The making of a beautiful and lasting marriage takes work. But work doesn't have to be a drag, especially if you love what you are doing and who you are doing it with."

6. SHARED DREAMS AND/OR SHARED INTERESTS

Intimates with shared interests have more opportunities for conversation and mutual enjoyment. With a shared dream to strive for, intimates are less disturbed by everyday problems and major crises, and have more mutual concern.

7. APPRECIATION OF EACH OTHER

One woman observed: "If a good friend lends you a china cup, you take the best care of it—you wash it by hand, it's always dusted, always shines, it's handled with care. But as soon as that friend says that it is an old cup, so you can have it—it's yours now, it's your possession—you neglect it. You put it in the dishwasher; if it gets chipped you don't worry about it so much. If it does not belong to you, you take that much better care of it. Somehow in relationships, as soon as you feel that you have that person totally, I think you neglect him or her."

Appreciating each other seems simple. However, one of the most common complaints of partners is that they are taken for granted. In good relationships, intimates make an effort to value and appreciate each other, and they actively communicate this feeling.

If all people are different from each other in principle, they are more purely different in peak experiences ... whatever the word "unique self" means, they are more that in peak experiences. In the peak experiences, the individual is most here–now, most free of the past and of the future in various senses, most "all there" in the experience.

ABRAHAM MASLOW[1]

PEAK EXPERIENCES

chapter eight

Maslow described peak experiences as times of highest happiness, greatest fulfillment, or mystical bliss. He found these moments occurring in activities as diverse as creative endeavor, appreciation of nature, athletic accomplishment, parental experience, and religious experience.

This chapter focuses on the peak experiences that occur between a man and a woman. The examples come from my research and from my practice as a clinical psychologist. Before reading the chapter, I suggest that you try the following exercise:

FOR AT LEAST FIVE MINUTES, THINK ABOUT THE PEAK EXPE-
RIENCES YOU HAVE HAD WITH A MEMBER OF THE OPPOSITE
SEX. THESE ARE EXPERIENCES OF TOGETHERNESS, JOY, AND
CLOSENESS. THEY MAY RANGE FROM MOMENTS OF VOLCANIC
EMOTIONALITY TO EXPERIENCES AS SUBTLE AS THE FEELING
OF GENTLE SNOWFLAKES ON YOUR SKIN.

What did you feel?

Consider what your peak experiences tell you about yourself and your relationships. Are there patterns and connections in these significant encounters? Awareness of your peak experiences can help you gain appreciation of your potential.

Some individuals can't recall any peak experiences during the five minutes. If this happened to you, perhaps your standards are too high, or perhaps these special moments have become buried in the happenings of everyday life. Upon deeper reflection you may remember. Highly emotional "big bangs" stand out, but subtle experiences of togetherness, joy, and closeness, which are far more common, may not be recalled because of their lower intensity. Like mountaintops, peak experiences vary tremendously and lower ones, despite their beauty, may not stand out as clearly from their surroundings.

Even though your significant experiences have special individual meaning making them distinct and unique, some characteristics are common to most peak experiences. There is usually a feeling of being totally involved and focused in the "now-ness" of the experience, and fears temporarily disappear. Spontaneity is natural in this more receptive, more accepting, more caring state. The emotions of wonder and awe bring you a more favorable view of the world, and you become more yourself—the self you are capable of becoming. Exciting parts of you may surface, parts you had only vague awareness of and that may reveal untapped potential to you. A major peak experience becomes a permanent part of you and memories will be built around it.

An older couple reminisced about an experience they had had far in the past. "There was this night on the beach," she reflected. "We had a room, but we stayed on the beach all night and made love. Nothing else counted that particular time. The children weren't born yet, and his problems with his work were forgotten for a few hours."

During a peak experience, intimates feel closer together, while simultaneously each feels more complete as a person. One young man described reuniting with his girl-friend. "Holding each other throughout the night was beautiful. It was as if a deep hunger was being filled."

The experience comes naturally and feels right. Inhibitions, doubts, and controls melt away. Often there is quiet togetherness, similar to that described by a 19-year-old college student.

> The closest we have ever felt was one time when we were sitting in the middle of an open field surrounded by tall grass, way out in the country. We watched the rise of the moon and counted stars and listened to the sounds of the country night. It was very peaceful and calm. We were both totally relaxed and at peace with ourselves.

In contrast to experiences of great peacefulness, sexual episodes are usually emotionally intense. Considering the potential that sexual expression creates for passionate interchange, many people, not surprisingly, recall only peak experiences involving sex. These experiences can be enormously arousing, ranging from sex for its own sake under erotic circumstances to sex as the expression of deep love.

In our society, where sexual problems are estimated to occur in at least half of all marriages, sex can be a source of both very good and very bad feelings. A low might even precede a high, as illustrated by an experience Jim had when he was 24. Jim was about to have sexual intercourse for the first time. He cared deeply for his girlfriend and had been anticipating this moment. To his shock and dismay, he was unable to have an erection. But they spent the night together, and their lovemaking the following morning stands out as his most profound peak experience.

First experiences, with their potential for special impact, are frequently cited as peak experiences. For instance, the first time we: had sex, met his/her friends, met his/her family, really opened up to each other, were truly spontaneous, smoked pot, told each other we were in love, decided to get married, did something different sexually, had a baby, received a special present, went on vacation, spent a weekend away from the children. For some people the wedding day is a powerful emotional experience. How we feel about a situation is what's important.

You can feel as if you are experiencing a first, even though it is not. Wendy, a 26-year-old attorney, provides such an example. She enthusiastically revealed:

> We had been seeing each other a year and a half. Then he was in the Army and we only saw each other on weekends. It was the end of the weekend and he had to leave. I felt sad about his leaving. We had been making love all weekend. We were caressing very tenderly. As he entered me I felt I was being entered for the first time; I felt exactly like I was a virgin. It was very exciting and very loving. We felt very close and tender.

Many peak experiences take place after a separation from the intimate, and in some ways the return resembles a first experience. Emotions are heightened. Sex seems new. Conversation is stimulating, with much to share.

During an absence we often become aware of the intense feelings we have for our intimate, and as a result may appreciate this person more. Our anticipation of being together again creates additional excitement.

Separations occur in good relationships because of external circumstances such as military service, business travel, school, hospitalization, visits to family, and so forth. When a separation takes place because of marital problems, a different set of principles applies. The shock of the separation, at times, results in the strengthening of the relationship. The opposite, however, is more often the case.

The story of Ed Wylie (as we will call him) illustrates the rescue of a deteriorating marriage. Many principles described in this book are apparent in the decline and rise of the Wylies' relationship.

During the Wylies' seven-year marriage, intimacy had gradually declined. After two months of separation from his wife, Ed, a brilliant professor of engineering, wrote the following:

> I feel that our marriage deteriorated for two basic reasons. First, we are both very "nice" people, and thus allowed much resentment to build up over the years without expression. Second, after some bad experiences in high school and early college, I had pretty well decided not to let myself get deeply emotionally involved with anyone, and so got married primarily for intellectual and practical reasons. We are both seeing each other and a marriage counselor regularly, and as I think you will see from the peak experiences, things are improving dramatically.
>
> My top peak experience occurred a couple weeks ago when we were simply sitting on the couch discussing our courtship and marriage and where we had gone wrong. My wife was mentioning several dates she remembered—the day we met, the date of our first date, the day I gave her the engagement ring, and some of her feelings during our courtship and early marriage—when it really hit me how much she must have loved me then, when I was incapable of really loving anyone. I broke down and started to cry, telling her that the reason for the sadness was my feeling that we really could have made it then had I been able to return her love. We embraced and must have cried on each other's shoulders for ten to fifteen minutes without saying a word, feeling very close to each other. It was a tremendously moving experience for both of us.
>
> A second peak experience occurred just last night. We had been discussing two things. First we had been talking

about the possibility of moving back together soon—our reservations, hopes, fears, the possibility of a contract to spell out what we expected and to force periodic re-evaluations of the relationship. Second, we had done a pairing exercise of telling each other one thing we really liked and one thing we really didn't like that the other person had done over the past week. Afterward, we simultaneously reached out and held each other for a few minutes, both remarking that we felt very close.

The Wylies are now back together. Their intimacy has grown, and with their new commitment to risk, to communicate, and to work on their relationship, they have· an excellent chance of continuing to grow together.

THE IRONY OF PASSION

Passionate love sometimes occurs under conditions that would seem more likely to provoke aggression and dislike. In fact, you may have had a peak experience with a partner who also caused you much pain. Ironically, unpleasant emotional states—fear, rejection, frustration, challenge, and jealousy—can arouse intense feelings of passion even in well-adjusted people.

How can we account for this paradox? Elaine Walster, a psychologist doing research on love, has proposed a two-component theory explaining passionate experiences.[2] The first component is emotional arousal. Both unpleasant and pleasant emotional states facilitate passion by arousing the body. This heightened physiological activity increases the intensity of the emotional experience. If the second component, a suitable person, is available, then a passionate love experience may occur. In other words, by arousing the body, states of emotional agitation may bring about a passionate experience if the "right" person is there. More commonly, positive feelings such as sexual arousal, excitement, appreciation, discovery, and joy have the same facilitating effect.

The potential for strong feelings eventually to create passionate love in seemingly inappropriate partners is demonstrated in both movies and literature. In *The African Queen,* two unlikely people develop love for each other as a result of the challenge, excitement, and danger of their trip down the river.

A disturbing event may evoke a strong emotional reaction toward another person. The individual may experience the incident as being anywhere from intense hostility to intense attraction, depending on how he interprets his feelings. This principle applies even when the other person has done nothing to cause the event.

Elliot, a 52-year-old accountant, described the following as his most profound peak experience with someone of the opposite sex.

> Oddly enough, the thing that occurs to me was with my first wife. We were fishing off Panama City in this 14-foot racing boat I had. We were out enjoying the weather and the fishing and everything was fine. And we saw what looked to be a school of sharks coming toward us. By a school, I'd say, maybe three to six, something like that. You could see their fins come out at times. And when they got closer, we realized that they weren't sharks, but were three big manta rays. The "fins" were their wingtips coming up out of the water. I guess the biggest one was about 8 feet across, and here we were a couple of miles offshore in a tiny boat and these great big manta rays came up to within I guess 8 feet of the boat. That's real close!

The big manta rays could have sunk the boat. Elliot's fear aroused passionate feelings toward his wife that were unusual in his marriage. Sharing the danger enhanced togetherness. Elliot's ex-wife also feels that this was the peak love experience in their relationship. Theirs is an example of how passion evolved out of their response to danger.

Just as danger activates emotions, a conflict between intimates can also arouse strong feelings. If the disagreement is dealt with effectively, then great closeness might occur afterward.

MORE GOOD EXPERIENCES

A change in routine may renew togetherness. Couples frequently report feelings of closeness during a vacation. Even a weekend away from the children can be enlivening. One couple fondly recalled the peaks of pleasure from a weekend at a nearby motel, while the children were at their grandparents' home.

Taking on a new role may provide fresh opportunities for intimacy. Reversing roles can originate from a planned exercise for the fun of it, or can be forced upon the couple by outside circumstances. Ellen, a 36-year-old secretary and mother of two children, observed:

> When my husband was recuperating after serious surgery on his spine and was confined to a body cast for several months, we had a lot of difficulty in our relationship. We were 24 and 27 at the time and I had the total responsibility for his care, bathing, feeding, and so forth, for this

period. I was pregnant and threatening a miscarriage. The first week was filled with argument and frustration. We had a talk and decided we had to make our situation more tolerable. The result was one of the happiest, closest experiences of our life together; we shut the world and our problems out. We stayed alone in our apartment, playing rummy, listening to music, and having conversations and sharing feelings in good humor such as we'd never had before. It was a new and different experience to be so isolated together. I could not leave him for more than 30 minutes. It was a marvelous feeling to know that we could give each other so much. It was like being stuck in an elevator with a stranger and discovering that you liked each other's company so much you forgot you were stranded. I suppose our experience was a natural one, but I have always felt it was unique and wonderful.

Up to this point in their relationship, Ellen had been dependent on her husband. Now taking charge for the first time, she transformed a seemingly unfavorable occurrence into a good experience. In a situation of forced togetherness, free of most distractions, this couple developed new ways for intimately relating to each other.

Peak experiences with the opposite sex need not be romantic in nature. Carol, a 43-year-old nurse, told the following:

I have a most vivid memory from my childhood of something I did with my father. He was very athletic. I guess I was about 4 or 5 years old. He used to take us swimming and picnicking at a place called Chain Bridge. It was a big, dammed-up creek. It had a bridge across made of rope. There was a diving platform and my perception of it as a child was that it was very high, though it probably wasn't. I would get on my father's back and hold him real tight. And then he would dive into the water. I could think of just how safe and exciting it was. It was a marvelous experience. I can still feel the water as we dived down and it rushed all over us. It felt like he was the most wonderful thing in the entire world then. He was really an exciting man.

Childhood memories of special moments with a parent may be transferred to a future relationship, as in the following example. Linda and Tony had been married for almost two years. Theirs was an intimate relationship with good communication and numerous peak experiences. The most profound one for Linda occurred shortly after her father's death.

I had been quite depressed for several weeks after my dad died. He had always been my favorite person in the world and I had beautiful memories of his spending long hours talking with me on summer evenings in the backyard. After his death, I thought I would feel empty forever. Then, one afternoon, my husband and I were on the back patio—it was warm, with a nice summer breeze. Tony had his shirt off and looked very strong and masculine. We were not talking much because, due to my own depression, I had not been very communicative for a long while. Tony had been patient and loving with me but it hadn't seemed to help. After a while, he got up and got the hose to water some new grass we had recently planted. He walked down to the terrace and stood with his back to me while spraying the fresh grass. Suddenly the odors of the summer evening, the sound of the hose, and the fine spray occasionally wisping across my face flooded me with memories of the strong, protective, secure feelings I had always felt in my father's presence. I looked at Tony from the back—his shoulders and arms looked so big and strong. And I realized at that moment that I still had someone to take care of me. I walked up behind Tony and put my arms around his waist—he was very warm and solid. Soft tears poured down my face against his back and he turned and held my head against his chest for a long moment while I gently cried. Neither of us said a word, but I think I felt more warmth and love toward him in that moment than ever before.

Despite the transient nature of an occurrence like this, it can create deeper recognition of the intimate. Linda, as a result of this moving personal event, found greater love for Tony.

Abraham Maslow, a psychologist who spent much of his life studying peak experiences and self-actualization, observed that as he grew older his own peak experiences became both less intense and less frequent. This might be nature's way of protecting an older body which can no longer stand the extreme emotional arousal. Perhaps as novelty wears off, the highs and lows become modulated, and a person reaches a higher level with frequent little peaks of longer duration. Maslow refers to this more serene appreciation of the beauty and of the miraculousness to be found in ordinary existence as a "high plateau experience."

For many people, plateau experiences become more common in the later stages of their lives. The plateau has the awe, mystery, and surprise of the peak experience, but the elements are elevated rather than climactic. There is more tranquility and less emotionality. The plateau experience feels very good and is miraculous in a peace-giving, secure way.

Jane and Bernard, grandparents in their late fifties, have many opportunities for excitement. An active business and social life, mutual interests in art, and trips in their private plane provide much variety in their lives. One might expect their peak experiences to have an air of glamour, because their lifestyle offers ample opportunity for "big bang" occurrences. Yet, Bernard reports the following recurrent plateau experience as his most moving.

When we're at home in the evenings, Jane spends most of her time quietly humming in the kitchen while preparing dinner. Our den is an extension of the kitchen and I can sit in a big easy chair where we can see each other. We usually have the stereo on and I peruse the newspaper while she cooks. She likes to cook and finds it relaxing. We usually have a drink about this time, sharing our separate togetherness and once in a while we talk a bit between long periods of quiet. Sometimes I look up and just watch her from the back while she's chopping some vegetable or something. We both feel very content and relaxed at this time and very far away from the rest of the world. It's at these times that I think how very much I love this woman who has struggled with me through all my early years and raising our three kids. I think these are the most important moments we share.

Good marriages generate many plateau experiences which, unlike peak experiences, may be easily forgotten. Plateau experiences increase with the years, while peak experiences usually diminish. People who search for "big bangs" become disillusioned when they compare their good hours with the great emotional moments of the past.

A woman's sexual orgasm might provide an analogy. The woman who moderately enjoys sex may experience orgasms that stand out strikingly. But many very passionately sexual women often cannot tell when they actually have an orgasm.

Maslow concluded a discussion on plateau experiences with the following words:

It happens that frequently in looking for the high, a young man and a young woman meet and they have a very good sexual experience. It's a party atmosphere, you know, a high. It's wonderful. And then they say they fall in love. The first time she gets a cold and her nose dribbles, the whole thing is lost because they expected the relationship to stay at that high.

Too many young people delude themselves with the big bang theory of self-actualization. One of our tasks is to communicate better with young people and give them a greater appreciation of patience and for the miraculous elements in ordinary existence.[3]

Even though the strange and unusual may provide a shortcut to peak experiences, the important discovery is that two people can create these events in their daily lives. Peak and plateau experiences can make life rewarding. By becoming aware of them and by basking in them, we can develop feelings of aliveness and well-being. This appreciation is far better than searching for the highest peak of all while being oblivious to the beauty of the mountains all around.

In his article "Why Good Marriages Fail," Richard Farson says a major source of discontent is the comparison of the marriage with its own good moments. Couples lucky enough to have these good times find themselves unable to sustain them, and often find themselves unwilling to settle for ordinary times. But to avoid the valleys, it is necessary to eliminate the peaks.[4] People with unrealistic expectations cannot win, for nothing is ever good enough.

An interesting phenomenon occurs as we develop greater appreciation of pleasure and contentment. Not only does our happiness increase, but we keep finding *more* pleasure and contentment. Frequently it becomes apparent that certain attitudes make us more receptive to the pleasurable potential of our intimate relationship. There are other beliefs and fears, often held by unaware people who somehow do not see the miraculous happenings around them, which block this potential. The final section of this chapter has a mini-test designed to encourage the exploration of advantageous attitudes.

QUIZ: YOUR INTIMATE EXPERIENCE POTENTIAL

Below is a list of ten statements. Indicate whether you think they are true or false and base your answers on your actual or ideal intimate relationship. These items explore your potential for peak, plateau, and favorable experiences with your intimate.

1.	One of the partners always gets used or exploited in an intimate relationship.	True	False
2.	My pleasant experiences become more pleasant when they are shared with my intimate.	True	False
3.	I believe simultaneous orgasm is necessary for the enjoyment of sex.	True	False
4.	I believe that male and female roles should be clearly defined.	True	False
5.	I believe that telling inner feelings destroys the magic of love.	True	False
6.	I admit to being sexually attracted to members of the opposite sex other than my partner.	True	False
7.	My partner should accept me as I am, and not try to change me at all.	True	False
8.	I can really be myself with my intimate.	True	False
9.	We sometimes laugh and joke during sex.	True	False
10.	I respect my partner for allowing me to know his or her faults.	True	False

ANSWERS

1. *False*. A person can be, but is not usually, exploited in an intimate relationship. Being used or manipulated becomes less likely when you apply the material in this book to your situation.

2. *True*. The pleasure of sharing can become more important than what is being shared. Delight is enhanced by your intimate's satisfaction with the experience. Loving people often derive as much pleasure from their intimate's pleasure as they do from their own.

3. *False*. Performance standards may make sex a job to be done. The fun, spontaneity, and playfulness of sex are sacrificed to achieve unrealistic perfectionism.

    Despite publicized misconceptions, few sexual acts actually culminate in simultaneous orgasm.

4. *False*. The ability to transcend the limitations of rigid roles in daily life and in love increases your potential for meeting situations with full human involvement. For example, by being both an active and passive lover, you increase your capacity for excitement.

5. *False*. Sharing inner feelings allows you and your intimate to become closer to each other. It develops trust and understanding. There can be special delight in sharing secrets.

6. *True*. This indicates a healthy acceptance of yourself and of members of the opposite sex. Although self-actualizing lovers are more monogamous than the average, and relatively less driven to outside love affairs, they are much more free than the average in admitting sexual attraction to others.

7. *False*. Having impact on someone else makes us feel alive and important. It is unfair to try to substantially change your intimate, but an unwillingness to make even the slightest change is unreasonable.

8. *True*. Intimacy, spontaneity, and security flourish when you can be yourself in a relationship. There is no need to be guarded or to try to impress.

9. *True*. Sex, even though it often produces great peaks of ecstasy, can also be compared to the games of children and puppies. It can be cheerful, humorous,

and playful. Laughter during sex can be as appropriate as panting.

Quite simply, sex is fun and does not have to
always be passionate.

10. *True*. When you and your intimate share weaknesses,
defensiveness decreases while honesty and spontaneity increase. Love is more powerful when the intimates
are fully known to each other.

Intimacy flourishes in an accepting atmosphere.

Your potential for favorable experiences with your
intimate is:

Number Right	Potential
10	Excellent
9	Very Good
7–8	Good
4–6	Fair
2–3	Poor
1	Very Poor

If your score is lower than you would like, don't be
discouraged. This book is designed to increase your potential
for intimacy, and as you practice the principles described,
your capacity to love and be loved will grow.

*Love and eggs are best when
they are fresh.*

A RUSSIAN PROVERB

*Perfect love sometimes does not come till
the first grandchild.*

A WELSH PROVERB

GROWING TOGETHER

chapter nine

Here are some answers people gave to the question, "What advice about growing together can you give to a young couple"?

I have a vital message for young couples who look forward to dwelling together. And that is—I've found, through experience, that you should always leave a little space open for change. Because, without knowing or even dreaming, the often so-called perfect relationship is the quickest to crumble when the slightest, yet inevitable, change occurs.

A 21-YEAR-OLD MAN

I think the biggest piece of advice I could give to any man or woman fixing to get married is to get yourself together. If you know where you are and you know how you feel on certain values, then you can cope and you can relate and you can solve any problem that comes up. Also, marriage is constant work and you can never take your partner for granted or believe that it's going to be a constant bed of roses. No matter how strong a relationship you have, there are going to be some lumps in it, but the good times are worth it.

A 33-YEAR-OLD WOMAN

Marriage should be a commitment between one man, one woman, and God, to a life of mutual love, trust, respect, and consideration for each other, regardless of whether the actual ceremony is performed in the largest cathedral in the country, or by jumping over a broom in front of friends. Happiness in marriage as elsewhere is a state of mind. It depends more upon how one feels about it than on external conditions. It can be compared to a joint savings account in a bank—how much you get out depends upon how much you both put in. When both enter into a marriage with thoughts of giving and what he or she can give to a marriage rather than what he or she expects to get out of the marriage, both are likely to have a happy marriage.

A 42-YEAR-OLD WOMAN

The great difficulty here is that young people, when they're planning to get married, don't come for advice. But if that rare couple would come to me and ask, "What advice can you give us for our relationship?" I would say first of all spend some time getting to know each other. Keep your distance. Stand back so you can see the other person, so that you don't lose your perspective. Say to yourself, "Do I really wish to stay with this person for a very long time? Do I really wish to commit myself here?" You've got to know each other.

A 53-YEAR-OLD MAN

There's a real need for young people who are entering into an intimate relationship to recognize the need for communicating feelings and not just thoughts. Too many people go into a marriage with the idea that communication is simple—"All we've got to do is talk." They don't realize the nitty-gritty of what is involved. Unless they can clarify and exchange their feelings, they're going to be in trouble. Get them to think about how they feel with "I feel . . ." statements. Young people should clarify their expectations before the marriage.

A 61-YEAR-OLD MAN

I had a good husband and we expected it to be a lasting union. I don't believe young people today go into marriage with the idea of it being a lasting thing. Back in the old days you married for life and that carries its own obligation with it. I think you have to put up with what you have to the best of your ability.

A 75-YEAR-OLD WOMAN

Tolerance and understanding and unselfishness are prime ingredients. Compatibility is the key word, and different people have different ideas about compatibility. But with it you can make a successful marriage; without it there are conflicts. It would be nice if they had a set of principles and they would both agree to them.

A 76-YEAR-OLD MAN

To always communicate with each other.

An 81-YEAR-OLD WOMAN

Most people like to give a young couple advice for growing together in an intimate relationship. This information can be helpful, but the fact remains that every relationship is different. Each contains a special blend of assets and liabilities.

Psychologist Daniel Levinson writes, in his book *The Seasons of a Man's Life:*

> Whatever the period in which marriage occurs, all marital relationships begin with some combination of strengths and problems. A couple is never fully prepared for marriage, no matter how long and how well the partners have known each other. Couples who settle early for a very limited relationship may find this sufficient for a while, but in time the discontents will erupt in gross conflict or will lead to a stagnant marriage. Continuing developmental work is required of individuals and couples in successive periods of the life course, if the marriage is to evolve in mutually satisfactory ways. The stability of marriage as an institution has traditionally been sustained by the binding forces of culture, religion, extended family and law—and, frequently, by the tacit acceptance of discreet extramarital relationships. In contemporary society, as the legitimacy of authority and the bonds of social integration are weakened, marital stability receives less institutional support and depends much more on the efforts of the spouses.[1]

Intimates produce their own marital stability by coping with changes and by redefining their relationship as they go through the various stages of their lives. A testing of commitment usually occurs early in a relationship and during stressful life periods. The testing can take the form of questioning the intimate directly about commitment, of asking for favors, or of creating problems so that the intimate's response can be assessed. For example, a wife's food cravings during pregnancy, particularly cravings that are difficult to satisfy, can be viewed as commitment testing. A husband's efforts to satisfy her may not only demonstrate his involvement, but may also increase it. Logically, it makes sense that commitment increase before the birth of a child, because a stronger dedication to the marriage will be useful, given the stress that children place upon it.[2] The higher the commitment between the intimates, the easier it becomes for them to lay down roots, to derive security from the relationship, and to cope with inevitable life crises.

CRITICAL STAGES IN A RELATIONSHIP

Some stages in the life and the relationship cycle are predictable, and some methods of coping are better than others. During the past several years, scientific research articles and books such as Gail Sheehy's *Passages* and Daniel Levinson's *The Seasons of A Man's Life* have described these important stages. This section will briefly discuss the critical stages in a relationship and methods of coping with them.

THE FIRST FEW YEARS

About one-half of all divorces occur during the first seven years of marriage. For second marriages, the majority of divorces occur during the first three years.[3]

Our society perpetuates unrealistic marital expectations. As a result, intimates usually have a romanticized concept of love and avoid fully discussing serious differences that will create future problems. They hope the excitement of the first year will continue. They expect marriage to make them happy and to satisfy their romantic needs, their sexual needs, their communication needs, their financial needs, their esteem needs, and their social needs. Living together on a day-to-day basis shatters the illusion.

The first few years of living together place many demands on the couple. They must face unmet expectations, everyday problems, loss of individual time, lessened romance, and unpredictable changes. And the situation becomes more complicated if they have a child.

Children. For many couples, the birth of a first child is a peak experience.

> The most joy, closeness, and togetherness I have ever felt was when we had our first child. I will never forget the exhilaration I felt when I watched my husband hold his son for the first time and inspect him, and the marvelous feelings we felt for each other. That was the most communicative my husband has ever been.

But rearing children can be a hard, time-consuming, nerve-wracking job. In a study of a large random sample of married people, Karen Renne found that couples who were in the process of raising children were more likely to be dissatisfied with their marriages than couples who had never had children or whose children had left home, regardless of race, age, or income level.[4] Another researcher found that couples whose children were young felt the most stress and pressure, and the pressure was greatest for the mothers.[5]

The following account by a mother of three children points out how the stress of parenthood can undermine a good relationship.

> I graduated from college and was on my way to a playwriting career. I met an exciting man who is now an

outstanding scientist. We fell in love—that is, we loved to be together, we loved to talk, to dream, to make love. We were alive and felt the world was our oyster. After we married, nothing tarnished. Our sex life was better than ever; our talks more meaningful. What's all this talk about unhappy, meaningless marriages, we wondered. Then, joy of joys, I got pregnant. And believe it or not, I had twins. Two years later I had a third child. Suddenly I was catapulted into a world I hadn't chosen—diapers, laundry, scrubbing floors, doctors, shopping, cooking, cleaning and over and over again. Suddenly I was overwhelmed with "THE MECHANICS OF LIVING" while Bob continued in his world of science and esoteric academic living. Of course, I made him pay—I screamed and tortured him at night; so much so he started working late two or three nights a week. . . .[6]

Our society paints a romantic picture of parenthood. If intimates will also look at the other side—the psychological and material costs of being a parent—they will be better prepared to deal with the problems and pleasures of raising children. Writer Judith Viorst, mother of three children, says:

How, women ask, can children enrich a marriage when they restrict your freedom, interrupt your conversations, invade your bedroom, deplete your bank account, exhaust your body, shatter your nerves and break your best wineglasses? How, women ask, can children enrich a marriage when your husband, since they arrived, is always complaining that you never have any time for him and also is always complaining that the house is a mess? How, women ask, can children enrich a marriage when all they provide is a whole new subject to fight about? Is it not true, as I read in a book called *Mother's Day Is Over,* that "the marriage that is *enhanced* by children is truly rare, the marriage that remains intact a monumental achievement"?

I don't deny that this may be the truth for many marriages, but it isn't the truth for the marriages I know. For most of the women I've talked to, including myself, believe that children *add* to the pleasures of marriage in spite of the messes and stresses and strains and restrictions and expenses that accompany them. Why? Because if shared experiences like travel or bowling or Bach or playing cards or fishing or collecting antiques can help to bind a marriage closer together, then surely a child, who binds us together in so many different ways—emotionally, biologically, historically—has to be the ultimate shared experience.[7]

THE CRISIS AROUND AGE 30 AND THE SEVEN-YEAR ITCH

Psychiatrist Ellen Berman studied this period of increased marital restlessness and tension. She and her colleagues found that a number of couples in the 27 to 32 age range coming to a large Philadelphia clinic for marriage counseling was *double* that of any other age range. Furthermore, these couples in the 27 to 32 age group had been married for an average of seven years. Usually, both partners felt at least some restlessness and the need for a reevaluation of their relationship.[8]

During the age 30 crisis, which usually occurs between 28 and 32, the partners have a persistent feeling that they want more for themselves, more for their relationship. They think about what they want to do, rather than what they "should" do or are expected to do. New thinking challenges the restrictive framework of the past. Suppressed parts of the self emerge, and the need to re-evaluate life within this new perspective develops.

The re-evaluation will be most effective if the intimates admit and discuss how they have failed to reach their ideal expectations, facing any anger, resentment, and disappointment they feel. To clear the way for compromise and allow for personal growth, it is important that couples confront disillusionment directly, admit mistakes openly, and be willing to accept responsibility for what has happened. If intimates can work through their feelings during this stage, a stronger, more committed relationship can result.

SWITCH 40

"It is not hard to imagine what will happen when the husband discovers his tender feelings and the wife her sharpness of mind," wrote Carl Jung.[9] Many men in their early forties change their focus; some of the energy that was previously poured into career advancement now becomes channeled into the development of a more tender, feeling, ethical self. Women, coming to this inner crossroads earlier than men, will often evaluate their career options at around age 35. This can be an exciting time for a women as she becomes more assertive and explores educational and occupational possibilities. Men going through this stage are able to look beyond illusions and facades, and to see new parts of themselves. They become more interested in love and tenderness. During an interview with Gail Sheehy, a famous television newscaster exposed his feelings.[10]

> "Why in the hell do we have so much trouble with the opposite sex?" he exploded. "The most important thing to a man next to his job, and even higher than his job if he really will admit it"—the newscaster paused, being of an age when he finally could admit it—"is the personal relationship with his woman. Why is that the area he's dying in?"
>
> "Men are not given awards and promotions for bravery in intimacy," I commented.

"And I'm angry about it." He jumped to his feet, forgetting the portrait, forgetting everything but the urgency to express a neglected side of himself. "We get accused of being untender and ungentle, and we're not all those things," he insisted. "The other side never got a chance to grow. All we heard about was drive, success, work." By the illustration he then gave, it was clear that he was trying, at 46, to be comfortable in letting out these new feelings.

"I can go out on a city street and yell at the top of my lungs, 'I hate you, you s.o.b.!,' and nobody will turn around, right? But get out there and start yelling 'I love you!,' and fifteen people will stop in their tracks as if I just held up a bank." He smacked a fist against his palm. "That's not right!"

THE EMPTY NEST SYNDROME

A 62-year-old man says:

As the children got grown and only one was left, we became afraid of being together alone. We realized we'd be facing life alone. We had a family togetherness concept and for years went camping together. We did a lot of things with the children.

But even though they're now gone, we still keep in close contact with them—you should see our phone bill. I think when any couple is faced with the prospect of being alone for the first time in twenty five years without the mutual responsibility of the children, it creates the need for a re-evaluation. Where do we want to go? What do we want to do? We've developed interests to take the place of what we did with them.

The departure of children can open up new possibilities for the intimates. By anticipating this life stage, and by pursuing old interests and developing new ones, the empty nest period can become a time of fulfillment.

TWO WOMEN–
TWENTY YEARS–
THREE MARRIAGES

Every relationship, despite predictable stages, is unique. This is apparent as two different women describe the crises with which they coped during their marriages.

Martha, a 39-year-old librarian, reflects.

> I was married in 1960 and from the beginning there was mutual support and love and acceptance. It is a rare thing to *be* happy, and even rarer to *know* you are happy at the same time. We were. But maybe the dice were loaded in our case because from the start we knew it wouldn't be forever. You see, three months before we were married, my husband, then a senior at Virginia Tech, discovered he had cancer and was given three months to live. We beat those odds by thirteen years and were able to make a paradise out of the time we had together. Does it count that as he died my husband still felt we were the luckiest people on earth? "How many other people do you know," he asked, "who in thirteen years wouldn't live any day differently?"

> My husband's life and philosophy would make a great column sometime. He was quite a guy and an inspiration to many others. He believed it is the *way* a man meets his fate and lives his life that counts—not what happens to him along the way. Instead of "why me?" his attitude was "why *not* me?" Most of the men who worked with him

didn't even know the burden he carried. Despite his death sentence, he went on to graduate with honors, work for duPont in Delaware a couple of years, and to return to Tech and get a Ph.D. (had a major recurrence while an uninsured and poverty-stricken grad student). Then we went back with duPont and he sent me back to college to get my degree. Meanwhile, we had two beautiful children (now 15 and 9) since researchers claim this type of cancer is not hereditary. After a few more duPont moves around the country, the final battle came four years ago, and he chose to fight with all that was available, all that surgery and chemotherapy could offer. He said he did it for me, so I'd never look back and wonder if we'd tried everything we could, and did it to add a grain of sand to the statistics—whether plus or minus—because it gave a little more meaning to it and might help someone else. I was with him night and day in a Houston hospital for twelve weeks. (Try living in a cancer ward some time— even in good health. You learn a lot about living from the dying.) I never saw him lose his optimistic outlook toward life *and* death, or lose his sense of humor. He lost the battle, but he won the war!

Me? I dropped the ball for a while. I married again a year later "to keep from being lonely" and found out what *real* loneliness is. We were both marrying for the wrong reasons, had no similar interests and goals, and were both still bleeding from past wounds. We were divorced over a year ago. Now I know about both sides of marriage.

Joyce, a 42-year-old mother of four children, tells of different crises during her twenty years of marriage.

I have been married for twenty years. Out of this union have come four difficult teenagers. Neither of us has been married to anyone else, nor have we ever seriously considered that as a viable option. Sometimes I am happy; sometimes I am miserable, sometimes I know I make my husband miserable, and vice versa. I think what I am trying to say is I no longer expect my partner to provide me with happiness, which takes him off the hook and places me upon it. Perhaps the difficulty comes in expecting marriage to *provide* happiness, not such an unlikely expectation in a consumerist culture. If Brand A doesn't work, try Brand B.

Certainly, when we got married, back in the romantic fifties, we had every expectation of living happily ever after. After all, together we had chosen our china and silver patterns, with perfect agreement in taste, we were provided the blessing of both families and the minister who performed the ceremony, and flew off for a honeymoon provided by our parents, in a cloud of tulle, rice, and romance. Early on this marriage was doomed. I vomited throughout the honeymoon, figuring (erroneously) I was allergic to my new husband, discovering too late we had neglected to purify our drinking water in our lakeside Canadian honeymoon cottage.

Since then, the relationship has been fraught with every possible kind of disaster: too many babies too fast, too many moves from place to place while my husband pursued his medical training, my own martyred response to his professional success while I rinsed diapers, without, mind you, the support of a women's movement to suggest some of my unhappiness might be legitimate. I felt guilty about my negative feelings, which is a real bind.

Twenty years later, I find myself feeling strongly enough about this difficult relationship to write about it. I'm wanting to tell you we both value it enough to fight for it. Recently we made an agreement that we both owe it to each other to fight, when we do with each other, with all our strength. That comes from knowing the value of fighting, the kind of growth that can result from struggling with another person. At times we have sought professional help, and believe in this.

The romantic myth is that marriage provides happiness. Wouldn't it be nice if we could so easily complete ourselves! Marriage *does* provide one other person who knows you well, someone to help parent your children, and—a recent revelation for us—a sense of rootedness and security that I find stabilizing in an otherwise unstable, alienated world. It's kind of nice to have someone around who's been there ever since I've been an adult—who can acknowledge me as a changing person.

Marriage is like long-distance running. It takes discipline, endurance, and perseverance as one suffers through the early discomforts of shin-splints, aching muscles, and fatigue. Only a few dedicated souls make it to the stage where they experience the payoffs of running: a sense of well-being, superb physical endurance, sometimes euphoria. Any runner knows there is no easy way to get there.

GROWING WITH YOUR INTIMATE

An intimate relationship can be a great source of happiness, inspiration, and growth. And like a kaleidoscope, its patterns will keep changing. Whatever the nature or the course of your relationship, you can be sure that it will change, and that it will demand choices and decisions from you. The information in this book, used effectively, can help you and your intimate grow together. The potential for growth is always there; the choices are yours to make. I end this book with the following passage for you and your intimate to share:

Every moment that we are together, I am learning something, and that knowledge becomes a permanent part of me. Everything we share and communicate becomes a permanent part of my growth process. Though my feelings will be different a year from now, or ten years from now, part of the difference is you. Because of you, I am a different person, and the person I will grow to become, with or without you by my side, will have gotten there partly because of you. If you were not in my life right now, I could not be who I am right now. Nor would I be growing in exactly the same way. Much of what I grow toward, and change within myself, has to do with what I respond to in you, what I learn from you, what I perceive about myself through you, and what I learn about my feelings in the dynamics of our relationship. I do not worry about our "future together," since we have already touched each other and affected each other's lives on so many levels that we can never be totally removed from each other's consciousness. A part of me will always be you, and a part of you will always be me. That much is certain, no matter what else happens.[11]

NOTES
AND OTHER
REFERENCES

INTRODUCTION

NOTES

1. Erich Fromm, *The Art of Loving* (New York: Harper & Row, 1956).
2. "Proxmire's Not Smitten with Research on Love," *United Press International,* March 1975.
3. Robert Hazo, *The Idea of Love* (New York: Praeger, 1967), p. xi.

OTHER REFERENCES

ROSENMAN, MARTIN F., "Intimate Relationships and Mental Health," in Robert A. Kronley, ed., *Exploring Mental Health Parameters,* Vol. 2. Atlanta: Darby, 1976.

CHAPTER 1

NOTES

1. Morton M. Hunt, *The Natural History of Love* (New York: Alfred A. Knopf, 1959). Reprinted by permission of the author.
2. John Alan Lee, *The Colors of Love* (Englewood Cliffs, N.J.: Prentice-Hall, Inc., 1976), p. 69.
3. W. Somerset Maugham, *Of Human Bondage* (London: Penguin Books, 1963), p. 607. Reprinted by permission of the Estate of W. Somerset Maugham.
4. Lee, *The Colors of Love,* p. 90.
5. Ibid., p. 135.
6. Magnus Hirschfield, *Sex in Human Relationships,* trans. John Rodker (New York: AMS Press, 1975; reprint of the 1935 edition published by J. Lane, London).
7. Lee, *The Colors of Love,* p. 20

OTHER REFERENCES

HATKOFF, T. S., "Cultural and Demographic Differences in Persons' Cognitive Referents of Love" (doctoral dissertation, University of Southern California, 1978), *Dissertation Abstracts International,* 1978.

LASSWELL, T. E., and M. E. LASSWELL, "I Love You But I'm Not In Love With You." Presentation at the meeting of the American Association of Marriage and Family Counselors, Toronto, 1975.

LASSWELL, MARCIA, and NORMAN LOBSENZ, *No-Fault Marriage.* Garden City, N.Y.: Doubleday, 1976.

LEE, JOHN ALAN, *Colours of Love.* Toronto: New Press, 1973.

———, "The Styles of Loving." *Psychology Today,* October 1974, pp 44–51.

———"A Typology of Styles of Loving," *Personality and Social Psychology Bulletin,* 3 (1977), 173–82.

ROSENMAN, M. F., "Love—Can It Be Measured?" Presentation at the meeting of the Southeastern Psychological Association, Atlanta, 1978.

———, "Liking, Loving, and Styles of Loving," *Psychological Reports,* 42, (1978), 1243–46.

RUBIN, ZICK, "Measurement of Romantic Love," *Journal of Personality and Social Psychology,* 16 (1970), 265–73.

———, *Liking and Loving: An Invitation to Social Psychology.* New York: Holt, Rinehart & Winston, 1973.

CHAPTER 2

NOTES

1. Oscar Wilde, *Phrases and Philosophies for the Use of the Young.* (London, England: A. Cooper, 1894).

2. Reprinted from *Handbook to Higher Consciousness* by Ken Keyes, Jr., 5th ed., Copyright 1975 by the Living Love Center, 1730 La Loma Avenue, Berkeley, California, 94709.

3. Don E. Hamachek, *Encounters With The Self,* 2nd ed. (New York: Holt, Rinehart & Winston, 1978), pp. 242–43.

4. Ron Hudspeth, "Cinderella Has A Ball and Gets Her Revenge," *The Atlanta Journal-Constitution,* 28, no. 72, (1978), 2.

5. Dag Hammarskjold, *Markings,* trans. Leif Sjoberg and W. H. Auden (New York: Alfred A. Knopf, 1972), p. 19.

6. Eugene C. McDanald, Jr., Bert Kruger Smith, and Robert L. Sutherland, "Self Acceptance," in R. L. Sutherland, *Understanding Mental Health* (Princeton, N.J.: D. Van Nostrand Co., 1965). Copyright © by Hogg Foundation for Mental Health, The University of Texas, 1962.

OTHER REFERENCES

DYER, WAYNE W., *Your Erroneous Zones.* New York: Avon Books, 1977.

ELKINS, DOV PERETZ, ed., *Glad To Be Me.* Englewood Cliffs, N.J.: Prentice-Hall, Inc., 1976.

JOHNSON, DAVID W., *Reaching Out.* pp. 145–48. Englewood Cliffs, N.J.: Prentice-Hall, Inc. 1972.

NEWMAN, MILDRED, BERNARD BERKOWITZ, and JEAN OWEN, *How To Be Your Own Best Friend.* New York: Random House, 1971.

PURKEY, WILLIAM, *Self-Concept and School Achievement.* Englewood Cliffs, N.J.: Prentice-Hall, Inc., 1970.

CHAPTER 3

NOTES

1. Merle Shain, *Some Men Are More Perfect Than Others* (New York: Charterhouse Books, Copyright © 1973). Reprinted by permission of the David McKay Company, Inc.

2. R. C. Robertiello, "The Occupational Disease of Psychotherapists," *Journal of Contemporary Psychotherapy,* 9 (1978), 123–29.

3. *New York Times,* November 10, 1965.

4. From the book PAIRING by George R. Bach & Ronald M. Deutsch, pp. 184–85. Copyright 1970 by Bach & Deutsch. Published by Peter Wyden. Reprinted by permission of the David McKay Company, Inc.

5. Reprinted from *A New Look at Love,* by Elaine Walster and G. William, copyright © 1978, by permission of Addison-Wesley Publishing Company, Reading, Mass.

6. E. Walster, G. W. Walster, J. Piliavin, and L. Schmidt, "Playing Hard-to-Get: Understanding an Elusive Phenomenon," *Journal of Personality and Social Psychology,* 26 (1973), 113–21.

7. Walster and Walster, *A New Look at Love.*

8. Reprinted from *Redbook Magazine,* January, 1977, p. 11, copyright © 1976 by the Redbook Publishing Company.

9. Helen Singer Kaplan in Carol Tavris, "When to Lie About Sex (And When Not To!)," *Redbook Magazine,* October 1978, pp. 123, 246–52.

10. Nancy Friday, *My Secret Garden* (New York: Simon & Schuster, 1973), p. 2. Copyright © 1973 by Nancy Friday.

OTHER REFERENCES

DERLEGA, VALERIAN J., and ALAN L. CHAIKIN, *Sharing Intimacy.* Englewood Cliffs, N.J.: Prentice-Hall, Inc., 1975.

ROGERS, CARL R., *Becoming Partners.* New York: Delacorte, 1972.

SEIDENBERG, ROBERT, *Marriage Between Equals.* Garden City, N.Y.: Anchor Press, 1973.

CHAPTER 4

NOTES

1. Oswald Schwartz, *The Psychology of Sex* (Harmondsworth, Middlesex, England: Pelican Original, 1949) p. 100. Copyright © the Estate of Oswald Schwartz, 1949. Reprinted by permission of Penguin Books, Ltd.

2. Barbara Walters, *How to Talk with Practically Anybody About Practically Anything* (New York: Doubleday, 1970), p. 166. Used with permission.

3. Jerry Gillies, *My Needs, Your Needs, Our Needs* (New York: Doubleday, 1975) p. 23

4. Dale Carnegie, *How To Win Friends and Influence People* (New York: Simon & Schuster, 1936), pp. 259–60, 263–65. Used with permission.

5. A. Fiore and C. H. Swensen, "Analysis of Love Relationships in Functional and Dysfunctional Marriages," *Psychological Reports,* 40 (1977), 707–14.

6. See David Mace and Vera Mace, *How to Have a Happy Marriage* (Nashville, Tenn.: Abingdon, 1977).

7. L. Navran, "Communication and Adjustment in Marriage," *Family Process,* 6 (1967), 173–84

OTHER REFERENCES

BRANDEN, NATHANIEL, *The Psychology of Self-Esteem.* New York: Bantam, 1971.

CALDEN, GEORGE, *I Count—You Count.* Nile, Ill.: Argus Communications, 1976.

HAUCK, PAUL A., and EDMUND S. KEAN, *Marriage and the Memo Method.* Philadelphia: Westminster Press, 1975.

HOPSON, BARRIE, and CHARLOTTE HOPSON, *Intimate Feedback: A Lovers' Guide to Getting in Touch with Each Other.* New York: Signet, 1976.

MILLER, S., R. CORRALES, and D. B. WACKMAN, "Recent Progress in Understanding and Facilitating Marital Communication," *The Family Coordinator,* 24 (1975), 143–52.

ROSENMAN, M. F., "Close Man–Woman Relationships and the Educational Process," *Resources in Education,* 1978, Document No. ED–155–277.

CHAPTER 5

NOTES

1. D. R. Mace, "Marital Intimacy and the Deadly Love-Anger Cycle," *Journal of Marriage and Family Counseling,* 2 (1976), 131–38.

2. Rollo May, *Love and Will* (New York: Norton, 1969), p. 148.

3. M. A. Straus, "Leveling, Civility, and Violence in the Family," *Journal of Marriage and the Family,* 1 (1974), 13–29.

4. C. Tavris and T. E. Jayaratne, "How Happy Is Your Marriage? What 75,000 Wives Say About Their Most Intimate Relationship," *Redbook,* 147 (1976), 90–92, 132–34.

5. See George R. Bach and Yetta M. Bernhard, *Aggression Lab* (Dubuque, Ia.: Kendall/Hunt Publishing, 1971); George R. Bach and Ronald M. Deutsch, *Pairing* (New York: Wyden, 1970); George R. Bach and Herb Goldberg, *Creative Aggression* (New York: Doubleday,

1974); George R. Bach and Peter Wyden, *The Intimate Enemy: How to Fight Fair in Love and Marriage* (New York: Morrow, 1968).

6. Richard B. Gehman, "The Vague Specific," *Collier's,* September 17, 1949, 71.

OTHER REFERENCES

BENJAMIN, ALFRED D., *The Helping Interview.* Boston: Houghton Mifflin. 1974.

CROSBY, JOHN F., *Illusion and Disillusion: The Self in Love and Marriage.* Belmont, Cal.: Wadsworth, 1976.

DAYRINGER, R., "Fair-Fight for Change: A Therapeutic Use of Aggressiveness in Couple Counseling," *Journal of Marriage and Family Counseling,* 2 (1976) 115–30.

GINOTT, HAIM G., *Between Parent and Teenager.* New York: Macmillan, 1969.

HOLT, R. R., "On the Interpersonal and Intrapersonal Consequences of Expressing or Not Expressing Anger," *Journal of Consulting and Clinical Psychology,* 35 (1970), 8–12.

O'NEILL, NENA, and GEORGE O'NEILL, *Open Marriage.* New York: Evans, 1972.

STRONG, J. R., "A Marital Conflict Resolution Model: Redefining Conflict to Achieve Intimacy," *Journal of Marriage and Family Counseling,* 1 (1975), 269–76.

CHAPTER 6

NOTES

1. Thomas S. Fee, "Let Us Walk Together," in *Love and Other Painful Joys* (Philadelphia: Dorrance, 1970).

2. Taken from "The National Love, Sex and Marriage Test," an NBC Television Special Event, Warren V. Bush Productions, Inc.; and Rubin Carson, *The National Love, Sex and Marriage Test* (New York: Doubleday, 1978), pp. 128–32. Used with permission.

3. Merle Shain, *Some Men Are More Perfect Than Others* (New York: Charterhouse Books, Copyright © 1973). Reprinted by permission of the David McKay Company, Inc. and the author.

4. William J. Lederer and Don D. Jackson, *The Mirages of Marriage* (New York: W. W. Norton, 1968), pp. 194–96.

5. The idea for the exercise is from Marcia Lasswell and Norman Lobsenz, *No-Fault Marriage* (Garden City, N.Y.: Doubleday & Co., 1976).

6. Ralph B. Hupka, "Societal and Individual Roles in the Expression of Jealousy," in H. Sigall (Chair), *Sexual Jealousy.* Symposium presented at the meeting of the American Psychological Association, San Francisco, 1977).

7. Gordon Clanton and Lynn G. Smith, *Jealousy* (Englewood Cliffs, N.J.: Prentice-Hall, © 1977), p. 11.

8. "Honest, Honey—It's All a Mistake." Chicago: *Associated Press: Newspaper Stories,* © Associated Press, 1976.

9. Larry L. Constantine, "Jealousy: Techniques for Intervention," in Gordon Clanton and Lynne G. Smith, *Jealousy* (Englewood Cliffs, N.J.: Prentice-Hall, Inc., 1977), pp. 190–98.

10. Karen Durbin, "On Sexual Jealousy," *The Village Voice,* October 18, 1973.

OTHER REFERENCES

BACH, GEORGE R., and RONALD M. DEUTSCH, *Pairing.* New York: Wyden, 1970.

O'NEILL, NENA, and GEORGE O'NEILL, *Open Marriage.* New York: Evans, 1972.

OLDS, SALLY WENDKOS, "How to Stay Close in Love without Losing Your Self," *Redbook Magazine,* April 1978.

SUID, R., B. BRADLEY, M. SUID, and J. EASTMAN, *Married, Etc.* Reading, Mass.: Addison-Wesley, 1976.

WALSTER, ELAINE, and G. WILLIAM WALSTER, *A New Look at Love.* Reading, Mass.: Addison-Wesley, 1978.

CHAPTER 7

NOTES

1. Vassilis Vassilikos, *The Plant, The Well, The Angel: A Trilogy,* trans. Edmund and Mary Keeley (New York: Alfred A. Knopf, Inc., 1964), p. 131.
2. *New York Times,* February 20, 1977, p. 16.
3. Eleanor D. Macklin, "Review of Research on Nonmarital Cohabitation in the United States," in Bernard I. Murstein, ed., *Exploring Intimate Life Styles* (New York: Springer, 1978).
4. Elaine Walster and G. William Walster, *A New Look At Love* (Reading, Mass.: Addison-Wesley, 1978).
5. Charles T. Hill, Zick Rubin, and Letitia Anne Peplau, "Breakups Before Marriage: The End of 103 Affairs," *The Journal of Social Issues,* 32 (1976), 147–68.
6. The idea for this exercise is from Barrie Hopson and Charlotte Hopson, *Intimate Feedback: A Lovers' Guide to Getting in Touch with Each Other* (New York: Signet, 1976), pp. 103–6.
7. See Jerry Gillies, *My Needs, Your Needs, Our Needs* (New York: Signet, 1975), pp. 27–28.
8. The idea for this exercise is from Gerald Walker Smith with Alice Phillips, *Couple Therapy* (New York: Collier Books, 1973), pp. 100–102.
9. As described in Fred Belliveau and Lin Richter, *Understanding Human Sexual Inadequacy* (New York: Bantam, 1970).

OTHER REFERENCES

CROSBY, JOHN F., *Illusion and Disillusion: The Self in Love and Marriage.* Belmont, Cal.: Wadsworth, 1976.

DOHERTY, W. J., P. McCABE, and R. G. RYDER, "Marriage Encounter: A Critical Appraisal," *Journal of Marriage and Family Counseling,* 4 (1978), 99–107.

FELDMAN, ELI, and SYLVIA FELDMAN, *Peak Sex.* Greenwich, Conn.: Fawcett, 1976.

GARRITY, JOAN, *Total Loving.* New York: Pocket Books, 1978.

HITE, SHERE, *The Hite Report.* New York: Macmillan, 1976.

HUDSPETH, RON, "Marital Bliss or Blister?", *Atlanta Journal,* 1977.

MACE, DAVID, and VERA MACE, *We Can Have Better Marriages.* Nashville, Tenn.: Abingdon, 1976.

McCARY, JAMES LESLIE, *Freedom and Growth in Marriage.* Santa Barbara, Cal.: Hamilton Publishing, 1975.

MILLER, HOWARD L., and PAUL S. SIEGEL, *Loving: A Psychological Approach.* New York: Wiley, 1972.

O'BRIEN, PATRICIA, *Staying Together: Marriages That Work.* New York: Random House, 1977.

POWELL, JOHN, *The Secret of Staying in Love.* Niles, Ill.: Argus Communications, 1974.

ROGERS, CARL R., *Becoming Partners.* New York: Delacorte Press, 1972.

ROSENMAN, M. F., "Human Sexuality and Relationship Counseling: A Workshop for Paraprofessionals," *Research in Education,* 10 (1975), ED-103–744.

SKOLNICK, ARLENE S., and JEROME H. SKOLNICK, *Family in Transition* (2nd ed.). Boston: Little, Brown, 1977.

CHAPTER 8

NOTES

1. From *Toward a Psychology of Being,* 2nd edition, by Abraham H. Maslow. © 1968 by Litton Educational Publishing, Inc. Reprinted by permission of Van Nostrand Reinhold Company.

2. Elaine Walster, "Passionate Love," in Bernard I. Murstein, ed., *Theories of Attraction and Love* (New York: Springer, 1971).

3. Stanley Kripner, "The Plateau Experience: A. H. Maslow and Others," *Journal of Transpersonal Psychology,* 4 (1972), 111–20.

4. Richard Farson, "Why Good Marriages Fail," *McCall's*, October 1971, p. 110.

OTHER REFERENCES

BACH, GEORGE R., and YETTA M. BERNHARD, *Aggression Lab*. Dubuque, Ia.: Kendall/Hunt, 1971.

FELDMAN, ELI, and SILVIA FELDMAN, *Peak Sex*. Greenwich, Conn.: Fawcett Publications, 1976.

MASLOW, ABRAHAM H., *Motivation and Personality*. New York: Harper & Row, 1970.

———, "Love in Healthy People," in Ashley Montagu, ed., *The Practice of Love*. Englewood Cliffs, N.J.: Prentice-Hall, Inc., 1975.

ROSENMAN, M. F., *Peak Experiences Between Men and Women*. Presentation at the meeting of the Association of Humanistic Psychology, Berkeley, 1977.

WUTHNOW, R., "Peak Experiences: Some Empirical Tests," *Journal of Humanistic Psychology*, 18 (1978), 59–75.

CHAPTER 9

NOTES

1. Daniel J. Levinson, *The Seasons of a Man's Life* (New York: Alfred A. Knopf, 1978), pp. 108–9.

2. Paul C. Rosenblatt, "Needed Research on Commitment in Marriage," in George Levinger and Harold L. Raush, eds., *Close Relationships*, pp. 73–86 (Amherst: University of Massachusetts Press, 1977).

3. *Data Tract 4: Households and Families* (Washington, D.C.: American Council of Life Insurance, 1978), p. 11.

4. K. S. Renne, "Correlates of Dissatisfaction in Marriage," *Journal of Marriage and the Family*, 32 (1970), 54–67.

5. Angus Campbell, "The American Way of Mating: Marriage Si, Children Only Maybe," *Psychology Today,* 8 (May 1975), 37–43.

6. N. K. Schlossberg, "Liberated Counseling: A Question Mark," *The Journal of the National Association for Women Deans, Administrators, and Counselors,* 38 (1974). 3–10.

7. From "The Messes, the Stresses, the Strains, the Joys . . . KIDS!", reprinted from *Redbook Magazine,* June 1976, p. 11. Copyright © 1976 by Judith Viorst.

8. E. M. Berman, W. R. Miller, N. Vines, and H. I. Leif, "The Age 30 Crisis and the 7-Year-Itch," *Journal of Sex and Marital Therapy,* 3 (1977), 197–204.

9. Quoted in Joland Jacobi, *The Psychology of C. G. Jung* (New Haven, Conn.: Yale University Press, 1973), p. 122.

10. See Gail Sheehy, *Passages* (New York: E. P. Dutton and Co., 1976), p. 31 (quoted passage, from p. 121, used with permission). Copyright © 1974, 1976 by Gail Sheehy.

11. Jerry Gillies, *My Needs, Your Needs, Our Needs* (New York: Doubleday, 1974), p. 211–12. Used with permission.

OTHER REFERENCES

AUSTIN, RICHARD B., *How to Make It with Another Person.* New York: Macmillan, 1976.

GOLDSTINE, DANIEL, KATHERINE LARNER, SHIRLEY ZUCKERMAN, and HILLARY GOLDSTINE, *The Dance Away Lover.* New York: Ballantine Books, 1978.

HOULT, THOMAS F., LURA F. HENZE, and JOHN W. HUDSON, *Courtship and Marriage in America.* Boston: Little, Brown, 1978.

LE MASTERS, E. E., *Parents in Modern America.* Homewood, Ill.: Dorsey, 1974.

MENCKEN, H. L., ed., *A New Dictionary of Quotations.* New York: Knopf, 1962.

SPENCE, D., and T. LONNER, "The 'Empty Nest': A Transition Within Motherhood," *The Family Coordinator,* 20 (1971), 369–75.

VAN DUSEN, R. A., and E. B. SHELDON, "The Changing Status of American Women: A Life Cycle Perspective," *The American Psychologist,* 31 (February 1976), 106–16.

INDEX